The Ethics of Research with Children and Young People

The Ethics of Research with Children and Young People

A Practical Handbook

Second Edition

Priscilla Alderson and
Virginia Morrow

⑤SAGE

Los Angeles | London | New Delhi
Singapore | Washington DC

First published 1995 by Barnardo's, this SAGE Publications edition published 2011

Reprinted 2011

SAGE Publications Ltd
1 Oliver's Yard
55 City Road
London EC1Y 1SP

201100097b

SAGE Publications Inc.
2455 Teller Road
Thousand Oaks, California 91320

SAGE Publications India Pvt Ltd
B 1/I 1 Mohan Cooperative Industrial Area
Mathura Road, New Delhi 110 044
India

SAGE Publications Asia-Pacific Pte Ltd
33 Pekin Street #02-01
Far East Square
Singapore 048763

Library of Congress Control Number 2010925036

British Library Cataloguing in Publication data

A catalogue record for this book is available from the British Library

ISBN 978-0-85702-136-6
ISBN 978-0-85702-137-3 (pbk)

Typeset by C&M Digitals (P) Ltd. Chennai, India
Printed and bound in Great Britain by
CPI Antony Rowe, Chippenham, Wiltshire
Printed on paper from sustainable resources

FSC
www.fsc.org
MIX
Paper from
responsible sources
FSC® C013604

CONTENTS

ACKNOWLEDGEMENTS

We are grateful to Professor Helen Roberts for commissioning the original version of this book, and to the children's charity Barnardo's for publishing the first two editions (1995 and 2004), and for allowing us to publish the third updated version with SAGE Publications. We would like to thank our colleagues and students linked to our international MA course programme, Sociology of Childhood and Children's Rights, for their many valuable insights, and we also thank Patrick Brindle and Jeremy Toynbee. We are grateful to colleagues around the world who have sent us examples for the book, and we regret that we did not have space to publish them all. However, we hope that we have managed to reflect the exciting and varied activities and changes that have taken place since 2004, and to offer some useful ideas for what promises to be further progress on the ethics of research with children and young people.

ABOUT THE AUTHORS

Priscilla Alderson is Emerita Professor of Childhood Studies at the Institute of Education University of London. She has been involved with medical research ethics committees for 30 years, and more recently with committees that review social research. She has advised on the writing of research ethics guidelines for a range of medical, nursing, social and psychological authorities, and worked for some years with CERES, consumers for ethics in research, which aimed to raise ethical standards in health care research. As a sociologist, she has researched many aspects of children's lives and rights, including research with premature babies, with children who have long term illness or disability, with young people across London, and rights in schools. Details of many reports are on www.ioe.ac.uk/ssru/. Recent work includes *Young Children's Rights* (Jessica Kingsley Publishers, 2008). She is writing a book for a Routledge series *Childhoods, Real or Imagined: An Introduction to Critical Realism and Childhood Studies*. She teaches on the Institute's MA course on the sociology of childhood and children's rights.

Virginia Morrow was Reader in Childhood Studies at the Institute of Education, University of London, until 2010. She is currently Senior Research Officer in the Department of International Development, University of Oxford. Children and young people have been the focus of her research activities since 1988. Her main research interests are sociology and history of childhood, child labour and children's work, children's rights, methods and ethics of social research with children; children's understandings of family and other social environments. She is the author of numerous papers and reports and she is a co-editor of *Childhood: A Journal of Global Child Research*, also published by Sage.

Introduction

Children and young people are now routinely asked about their views on many aspects of their lives. National and local governments, together with countless agencies and services for children, invest much time, effort and funding in seriously consulting children and inviting them to share in planning and evaluating services. The United Nations Convention on the Rights of the Child (1989) enshrines the rights of children to form and express views freely in all matters that affect them, their views being given due weight according to the age and maturity of the child (Article 12), and many of the Convention's other 54 articles concern respecting and including children. Gradually these rights are achieving more respect in the research and consultations taking place around the world, as recorded in governments' regular reports on their progress in implementing the Convention and the UN Committee's responses (see www. ohchr.org). However, research and consultations with and about children raise ethical questions. Addressing these questions can be crucial for the processes, methods and outcomes of effective research, and we will review the questions in the order in which they tend to arise during the ten main stages of each research study. As we explain later, instead of providing general answers, we aim to help people to think about the practical questions posed by their specific projects, and about possible ways to avoid or resolve ethical problems.

Defining some terms

We define *social research* broadly, to include any process that collects and reports the views and experiences of children and young people. We refer to 'research', 'study' and 'projects' in order to avoid lengthy lists of types of projects, which could include consultations, evaluations, audits, inspections and participatory projects, that all collect and report data, and can all raise ethical questions.

Besides using the traditional *methods and activities* of observations, questionnaires, case studies, interviews and group discussions, researchers may also ask children to take photos, or make diaries, maps and videos about their daily life. They may involve children and young people as researchers themselves, and the use of emails, chatrooms and social networking websites, such as Facebook, is increasing. We will review ethical questions raised by all these activities.

Social researchers are people of any age, who carry out any of these kinds of work. They may come from local or national government departments and services, commercial, independent or voluntary organisations, academic or practitioner and service user or activist backgrounds. They may be professional, student or 'lay' researchers, consultants or evaluators, journalists or market researchers. They may research in the natural or social sciences, the humanities, in IT or business studies. We count them as 'social researchers' if they are observing or talking to children and collecting data about their views or experiences. Social researchers may aim to add to knowledge, to evaluate goods or services, to inform and change policy and practice, and/or to promote children's participation and inclusion.

We hope that *readers* who will find this book useful will include people who design, fund, commission or manage research or consultation projects, as well as those who collect, process, analyse and report data. We are writing for researchers who apply to research ethics committees (RECs) or institutional review boards (IRBs) for ethics approval of their research, as well as REC and IRB members. We hope that the fast growing number of people who teach and learn about research ethics will also find the book useful. Another important group is those who read research reports and protocols and decide whether to accept – or reject – them, and perhaps to publicise and implement the research recommendations. Knowledge of ethics standards, and how researchers should refer to them in their reports, can help critical readers who include policymakers and practitioners, service users and their advocates, experts who review protocols for funders and papers for peer-reviewed journals. Knowledge of ethics can help readers when making informed assessments of research, and when considering potential impact in how research findings might be interpreted and applied in policy, practice, teaching and in further research.

We usually call people who are being researched *participants*, although this is a contentious word, and sometimes it is more accurate to say 'research subjects', if they are not properly informed or respected (Smyth and Williamson, 2004).

Although we discuss *children and young people* through the book, to make it as readable as possible we often, rather awkwardly, shorten this phrase to 'children' to mean everyone from birth and under 18 years of age.

We have aimed to write an *international* handbook on research ethics in every continent, so how should we describe the Northern — Southern — or Western–Eastern countries? Neither pair is an accurate contrast. Wealthy Japan is in the Far East. Australia and New Zealand are in the supposedly deprived South, and so are Brazil and China, which are rapidly changing from 'third world' to 'first world' economies, so we avoid writing about 'richer/ poorer' worlds. Later we will challenge the neo-colonialist assumptions that 'Western' ethics completely differs from 'Eastern' ethics. We have avoided the terms 'developed/developing worlds' for the following reasons.

In a book about ethics and research with children, we challenge the partly oppressive notion of the deficient 'developing' child who will one day become a 'fully developed' adult; these concepts are even more misleading in international politics, economics and research. It is patronising to assume that all countries should emulate the post-industrial 'developed societies', which are so imperfect; 'undeveloped' countries have ancient and sophisticated civilisations. It is unrealistic to imagine that everyone should live to the standards of the most 'developed' and militaristic countries, because that would require the resources of six or more planets. The 'developed world' has much to learn from more modest civilisations, instead of building up vast debts for the next generations to repay, another concern for ethics and childhood.

Yet we also hope to avoid implying that we in the UK can simply export and impose our own ideas about research ethics into any other country. We aim to recognise the very different common life styles between children living in the richest 17 per cent and in the poorer 83 per cent of the world's population. Although the terms are not yet very widely used, we have relied on the concepts of the *minority* and the (poorer) *majority world*, as a reminder that most children today live in disadvantaged ways that can raise particular questions about research ethics, and we can learn so much from them.

One of the clearest understandings of the living ethics of research with children, as a relationship and far more than simply a set of skills or ideas, comes from Tatek Abebe (2009: 461) studying life in the 'deep-seated poverty and harsh material deprivation' of Ethiopia. He gave food and gifts to the children, and they gave him gifts in return.

I became compelled not to detach myself from their circumstances ... reciprocal relationships have nurtured the research space in many fruitful ways ... reciprocity ... reflects how ethical spatiality is the product of interrelationships ... and that dominant ethical principles are actually lived in, reproduced and experienced by research participants through interactions.

Research ethics

Research ethics is concerned with respecting research participants throughout each project, partly by using agreed standards. Ethics standards are also designed to protect researchers and their institutions as well as the good name of research. Healthcare researchers have gradually developed ethical standards over the decades since the first international Code was agreed in the 1940s (*Nuremberg Code*, 1947). National systems of healthcare RECs or IRBs are now well established in many countries, providing informative websites, routine reviews of local research protocols, and funds to train members and administer committees.

Fairly recently, social researchers have been expected to observe ethical standards more formally. Student researchers make up another large group that is being drawn into formal ethics review processes. While healthcare ethics guidance is by no means perfect, and involves different kinds of risk and harm from those of social research, it offers useful ideas for thinking about and promoting ethics in social research and consultation in general. One aim of this book is to inform and promote more discussion among social researchers about these ideas.

The purpose of this book: starting from uncertainty and the question format

Research and consulting can involve asking and trying to answer hard questions. Even if researchers believe that they thoroughly know the whole topic area and the likely results, they have to be alert to new, surprising and challenging findings if the research is to be valid and worthwhile. Researchers therefore have to start from uncertainty.

When testing or evaluating welfare, teaching or psychological interventions, for example, researchers must admit honestly to themselves and to the participants that no one is yet certain how effective each new or even well-used intervention might be. Otherwise, if there is certainty, the research is not worth doing. Researchers may have to juggle honesty with trying not to arouse too much anxiety, especially when participants are also patients or other vulnerable service users.

In the questioning research tradition, therefore, the main purpose of this book is to raise questions for researchers to consider, for the following reasons.

The law tends to define minimum standards of conduct in order to prevent bad practice. However, ethics guidance serves to raise awareness and to encourage higher standards, mainly through posing questions rather than providing answers; though ethics offers methods of addressing these questions.

Social research covers a wide range of disciplines and professions, with different ways of thinking and working, and of relating to children and young people. Researchers therefore often need to ask themselves how best to apply general ethical standards to their particular work. There may not be a single correct or expert answer. Much depends on the context, the topics and methods of each study. This careful working towards the best or least harmful answer is part of ethical research, in a do-it-yourself and not simply a ready-made, off-the-peg approach.

There are agreed principles and detailed methods of applying ethical standards, but sometimes the principles can seem to be in conflict. For example, how can we enable children to be heard in research without exploiting them? Can we protect and shelter children without silencing and excluding them? Can we pursue rigorous enquiry without distressing them? Critics of formal ethics may argue that, in these dilemmas, no one principle offers a sound valid ethical base. Yet the dilemmas need not involve choosing between principles, because these are also largely complementary, and skilful research involves working out with participants how to balance the principles.

Ethical review includes asking about the advantages and disadvantages of each method, and how it is relevant to, and therefore efficient for, each project's aims and questions.

Ethical questions are woven through every aspect of research, shaping the methods and findings. Ethics involves thinking critically about this process, rather than arriving at an imagined perfect endpoint. There are well-used signposts to help to map the ethical journey, and many of these appear through this book as prompts, rather than directives, to help investigators to question and reflect. It can also be helpful to keep records throughout the course of a research study about ethical issues and how you tried to resolve them.

This book is meant to raise questions for individuals and groups, to promote informed debate, and to contribute to current developments in professional and public understanding of the ethics of researching with children.

Researchers as insiders or outsiders

The investigators may be 'insiders' examining their own practice or organisation or a service they provide. Or they may be 'outsiders' who visit the research sites solely in order to do their own project. Each position has advantages shown in the numbered pairs below.

Advantages of being an experienced 'insider':

(1) You already know the general background and the specific topic and setting well, and can rely on plenty of insider knowledge.
(2) You can probably start with direct, practical aims often intended to benefit your organisation.
(3) Access is likely to be quickly and easily arranged.
(4) You may already have trust, rapport and good working relations with the participants.
(5) You may find it easy to involve the adults and children you work with in planning, carrying out and contributing to the research.
(6) These people may therefore feel that they 'own' the project and are willing to support the process and findings.
(7) You may have time, contacts, opportunities and support for the vital final stages of putting the study findings into practice, such as by changing routines and policies in the organisation. This long hard stage is ignored in too many projects.

Advantages of being experienced 'outsiders':

(1) You should be expert in efficient methods of planning and conducting thorough research, on time and to budget. You may see vital issues that insiders overlook, and be more free to take the independent critical view that is vital to research.

(2) It may take time to work out the key aims. It is practical to work critically on questions instead of assumptions, such as asking who might or might not benefit from the research findings and what 'benefit' really means in this context.

(3) Access may be slow, but this may help to ensure that you have to inform everyone concerned, ask for their consent, and observe high ethical standards.

(4) You should be able to set up good working relations with participants quickly. You do not have a history of either good or poor relations with them, which can be an asset. They relate to you as a researcher, and not also sometimes as a colleague or service provider. Your independence might help people to talk to you more honestly about problems, and to expect you to be fair, open-minded and very careful about confidentiality.

(5) You have to spend much time talking with people about how they could be involved in the study. Yet this can help them to make informed unpressured decisions, and so be committed to their part in the research.

(6/7) If you gain their informed trust and respect, the participants might be willing to accept surprising and even unpopular research findings – even if your contract and budget end before you can work with them on applying the findings.

One way to combine these advantages is to have mixed teams of insiders and outsiders, though they will have to allow enough time for careful negotiations throughout the research, to do justice to their very different positions. Another way is to fund more time before and after the main data collecting and reporting stages, in order to support the work of involving participants at every stage from planning the research to implementing recommendations.

We suggest that it is vital that insiders are very clear, to themselves and everyone else concerned, when they are, or are not, 'wearing their research hat'. They could wear a 'researcher' badge, to show the times when more critical, challenging and confidential discussions are invited. To point out this crucial difference and independence, we therefore refer to everyone doing research, consultancy or evaluation of their own or other people's services as 'researchers'.

The contents of this book

To help you to find the issues you are interested in, the ten main chapters are based on 'Ten Topics'. These review practical ethical questions raised by social research and consultations from the early planning stages onwards. The Ten Topics are summarised at the end of each chapter. Some chapters will include extra material beyond the immediate practical concerns. Chapter 1 will briefly review the meaning, history, theories and practice of ethics in research. We have drawn ideas from national and international ethics guidelines, written for healthcare researchers and for social scientists, teachers and social workers, journalists and market researchers, and others. We suggest that some guidance may be too rigid and narrow, and so we raise the following questions.

- What can researchers learn from reflecting on their moral feelings and relationships during their research? (Chapter 3.)
- How can researchers complement traditional approaches in ethics with greater awareness of the interests, rights and abilities of children and other disadvantaged groups? (Chapter 4.)
- How do financial and professional pressures, time constraints, stress and many other daily practicalities affect each research project, and what ethical questions do such pressures raise? Should children and young people be rewarded for taking part in research? (Chapter 5.)
- How does the broader social context, including the values, politics and economics of society, affect research with children? (Chapter 6.)
- How can researchers give clear information (Chapter 7) and respect informed and freely given consent or refusal? (Chapter 8.)
- How does research affect all children, beyond the individual researcher–child relationship? What is the collective impact on children and young people when research reports influence public and media opinion and professional policies and practices? (Chapter 10.)
- How can individual researchers and research teams be supported when they try to resolve controversial questions in their work? Are research ethics committees helpful? (Chapters 6 and 11.)

This book also considers ethics during two stages of research that are often overlooked.

- The initial plans when setting up research teams, and possibly involving partici-pants as partners from the start (Chapter 4).
- The final stages after research reports have been published, of disseminating the findings widely, and working to link research into policy and practice (Chapters 9 and 10).

Chapter 11 summarises some practical suggestions for future policy for all concerned with social research with children and young people.

Throughout the text, we have included examples sent to us by researchers and others, or from published work. These examples are intended to show how others have tackled various problems, and to help our readers when thinking through some of the issues raised. These examples show how sensi-tive, transparent, valid research and consultation can be conducted when ethi-cal questions are clarified and checked, directly and indirectly, with other researchers, reviewers, and with the young participants themselves.

For this new edition of the book, we have emphasised international research more to try to reflect the burgeoning research with children in the majority world. Key new references are: Ennew and Plateau (2004), Laws and Mann

(2004), Schenk and Williamson (2005) and a special issue of *Children's Geographies*, with the introduction and papers by Beazley et al. (2009). In doing so, we do not want to overstate the differences between countries and cultures, because many of the questions that arise in research with children are global, to do with power, access and negotiations with gatekeepers. There is a danger of creating a false dichotomy between minority and majority worlds that we want to avoid. Research ethics always involves taking account of the local context and understandings of children and childhood, and child–adult relations, particularly in relation to power dynamics and how children are expected to obey adults.

This handbook is a resource in a time of quite rapid change when ethics guidelines are regularly revised and funders are setting new standards. So besides referring readers to books and reports, we cite websites that are often updated, including an online web-based guidebook for researchers that we have both been involved in developing www.ethicsguidebook.ac.uk.

PART 1

The planning stages

One

Planning the research: purpose and methods

Two basic questions

There are two basic ethical questions at the outset of any study, whether it is research, evaluation, audit or other consultation.

- Is it worth doing?
- Can the investigators explain the research clearly enough so that anyone they ask to take part can give informed consent or refusal?

These two questions lead on to many sub-questions, and this chapter begins by reviewing the sub-questions raised by a range of research purposes and methods. We then summarise three stages of growing awareness about research ethics. These are linked to three main ethical frameworks for assessing research studies based on ideas about duties, rights, and harms or benefits. The chapter ends by returning to the importance of starting from uncertainty.

Questions about purpose and methods

- Are the research questions worth asking and why?
- Have they already been answered – has previous research on this question been checked for in a thorough literature search?
- In whose interests are the questions being asked?
- How well do the methods fit the aims in order to conduct research effectively?
- Do the chosen methods offer the best, or at least the most reasonably efficient, means of answering the questions?
- What are the strengths and limits of the chosen methods?

Is the research worth doing?

Research, consultations and evaluations can be unethical in the sense that they ask the wrong questions, or the methods do not fit the questions. The studies may waste time and money, at best come up with useless answers, and at worst produce misleading ones that support future misguided and even harmful policies.

Do theories matter?

Research is often seen as either theoretical or practical. Yet it is not as simple as that. First, all research and questions are grounded in theories, as Box 1.1 illustrates. We cannot avoid holding beliefs or theories, for example, about what children are and ought to be like. For most of the 20th century, developmental psychology dominated the study of childhood and it tends to construct children as 'human becomings' rather than fully 'human beings' (James and Prout, 1997; Mayall, 2002; Qvorturp, 2005; Alderson, 2008).

It was not until theories about children's incompetence began to be questioned that research began to be funded and conducted which took more account of children's own experiences and capacities. When researchers accept theories of children as real people, this leads on towards more mutually respectful ethical relationships in research.

Box 1.1   Defining terms, thinking about theories: 'young carers' of a disabled family member

How many hours of care have to be given in an average week for a child to count as a 'young carer'? And how does that time differ from the housework and childcare and loving support that children give in so many families that do not have a disabled member? The way theories see children (and also disabled people) as victims or problem-solvers, as helpless dependents or else interdependent contributors interacting with other family members, will alter the research questions and conclusions.

Do viewpoints matter?

Researchers used to think that they could take a single overview that spoke for everyone. Yet there are always different ways of seeing and understanding children, which alter how children's accounts of themselves are elicited and interpreted. Each member of a family has a different viewpoint and, for example, children who 'play truant' from school or 'abscond' might have convincing reasons for doing so. Researchers therefore need to think about the 'standpoint' from which they are studying children, and the ethical implications of that standpoint: whether they try to stand in and understand the child's position or the adults' viewpoints, such as parent, teacher, social worker, politician or tax payer. Newer approaches involve respecting children's standpoints and competencies, and grounding research methods in this respect (Mayall, 2002). So a second ethical and useful way to examine theories, instead of taking standpoints for granted, is to be more aware of them and of the context, power differences and whose interests are likely to be served by the research (Box 1.2).

Box 1.2   Evaluating a school-based behaviour programme

A hypothetical example

A school invited a team to evaluate its behaviour programme, run by a specialist company, in which the 12 'most difficult' children in the school and their mothers took part in play and education sessions one morning a week. The team was asked to use a questionnaire to collect the views of the teachers, the parents and the programme company. The team decided to look at a wider range of views and alternatives as well. They asked all the children in the school what they thought about the effects of the programme, whether they thought there might be better ways to tackle behaviour problems, and how they might spend the budget for the programme. The children were much less likely than the adults to think that the programme worked well. They thought the play sessions and budget should be shared more fairly through the school, and they had positive ideas on how all the children and staff could work together to tackle the behaviour problems, instead of calling on outside help. The answers from different groups highlighted how people tend to speak from their own standpoint and interests. The 12 mothers were afraid to criticise the programme in case they seemed to endorse the view that they and their children were troublesome. The company praised the programme and so did the teachers who liked having one morning a week without their most difficult children. The 200 children in the school wanted to have more play programmes during their lessons.

Do methods matter?

Chapter 3 will review how each data-collecting method and source raises ethical questions on respecting the 'worth and dignity ... of all members of the human family' (UN, 1989). Mixed methods, for example, can help to include young children actively and respectfully (Box 1.3).

Box 1.3   The participatory Mosaic approach

Children aged three to four years took photographs, went on tours, and made maps and drawings while talking with adults (child conferencing), to build up a picture of children's perspectives on their early childhood settings and services. The researchers state that the 'framework for listening' is:

- *multi-method* in recognising the different 'voices' or language of children;
- *participatory* in treating children as experts and agents in their own lives;
- *reflexive* by including children, practitioners and parents in reflecting on meanings and interpretations of the data;
- *adaptable* because it can be applied in a variety of early childhood settings;
- *focused* on children's own experiences and views.

Information is gathered and then pieced together for dialogue, reflection and interpretation. The approach can be used for many purposes including looking at lives lived rather than knowledge gained or care received. It can be embedded into practice and used as an evaluative tool in individual reviews, internal audits, childcare audits, changes to the environment, promoting an ongoing dialogue, increasing confidence, developing skills and encouraging children to become more active participants. There is concern to listen carefully, to respect children's privacy and to avoid intruding into their free time (Clark and Moss, 2001).

Three phases in growing awareness of research ethics

This section outlines three phases of growing awareness about ethics in the longer history of healthcare research (Beauchamp and Childress, 2000), as a background to social research ethics.

Phase 1 – doing 'good' and feeling good: beneficence and duty

Early medical ethics guidelines were about etiquette, relations with colleagues and promoting public respect for the profession. Some of these standards benefited patients, but they also benefited the medical profession and its authority and power. In the Hippocratic tradition, from fifth century BC, doctors assumed they knew what was 'good' for patients (Box 1.4).

Box 1.4   Phase 1 – beneficence and duty: the main assumptions

- All true professionals fulfil their duty to benefit service users.
- Standards are ensured by training and expert knowledge.
- To be a professional means to be the best judge of what is good for your service users.

Phase 2 – concern about harm: respect and rights

Confidence in these beliefs was shaken by scandals about harmful research, such as the Nazi research that led lawyers to write the first international guidelines on ethical research, the *Nuremberg Code* (1947), which begins:

> 1. The voluntary consent of the human subject is absolutely essential [the ability] to exercise free power of choice, without the intervention of any element of force, fraud, deceit, duress, over-reaching or other ulterior forms of constraint or coercion.

Based on Anglo-American law, the *Code* respects personal integrity. Only people who are competent to consent should be asked to take part in research. Children were excluded as too vulnerable and pre-competent to be research subjects. Potential research subjects should be given enough information about the risks and hoped-for benefits to enable them to make 'an understanding and enlightened decision' about whether they wish to take part in research (Box 1.5).

Box 1.5   Phase 2 – concern about harm: the main assumptions

Research and services can harm as well as benefit.

- Professionals do not always act benignly.
- Professional expertise and self-regulation are valuable but not sufficient safeguards.
- Ordinary people can understand expert information if it is clearly explained.
- Only the potential research subject can make an 'enlightened' decision about whether to consent to research and take on the risks.
- Human rights must be respected.

Phase 3 – confidence yet caution: balancing harm and benefit

The *Declaration of Helsinki* (World Medical Association [WMA], 1964/2008) was the first international code on research ethics to be written by doctors, in response to public concern about dangerously under-researched medical treatments. *Helsinki* seeks to reassure by beginning with the doctors' expertise, and their mission to 'help suffering humanity'. There is only brief mention of 'informed consent', and instead the emphasis is on doctors' assessments of harms and benefits, of whether research is worthwhile, and of how to safeguard subjects' interests.

Medical research involving human subjects must be conducted only by individuals with the appropriate scientific training and qualifications. Research on patients or healthy volunteers requires the supervision of a competent and appropriately qualified physician or other health care professional. The responsibility for the protection of research subjects must always rest with the physician or other health care professional and never the research subjects, even though they have given consent. (Section 16 in the 2009 version.)

Slowly, doctors have acknowledged that they can make mistakes and cause harm and now they recognise that they have extra ethical duties to patients who take part in research. Yet unfortunately, examples of children as 'guinea pigs' in dangerous medical experiments continue to be reported (Sharav, 2003; Save the Children, 2007). Gradually the new discipline of bioethics, combining law, philosophy and healthcare, developed from the 1970s. Bioethics has spread into the networks of guidelines and research ethics committees around the world for healthcare research and later for social research (Box 1.6). Researchers are required to explain their work clearly enough to enable people to make informed unpressured decisions about whether to join a research project or not. We use bioethics ideas through this report, and comment on their strengths and limitations for social research (see Chapter 6).

A key point in bioethics is that doing research about children is very different from caring for them or teaching them. So, for example, teachers, play-workers or youth workers cannot simply do research with the children and young people they work with, as if the research is part of the service, and as if no one need ask for children's informed consent. Formal ethical standards are vital in all research studies.

Box 1.6   Phase 3 – confidence yet caution: the main assumptions

- Professionals have unique expertise and observe high standards.
- Professional knowledge must be tested and based on sound research.
- Improved professional regulation can promote ethical standards of research.
- Yet professionals must inform the people they research, and respect their views and decisions about whether or not to join the study.

We suggest that social research ethics has much to learn from the history of medical ethics and its guidance (see the References at the end of the book). Some large social research funders ask researchers to sign an undertaking that they will observe *Helsinki*. Among many clauses, *Helsinki* states:

- Researchers should give full information and request consent.
- All research on people should be reviewed by an ethics committee (see Chapter 6).
- Research protocols should always state the ethical considerations involved.
- Reports of research that has not been conducted in accord with *Helsinki* principles 'should not be accepted for publication' by journals.

Three ethics frameworks for assessing research

Three main working methods or frameworks in professional ethics are based on centuries of philosophical debate about *duty, rights, harm and benefit*. Box 1.7 shows how these three approaches differ, the strengths and limitations of each approach and the questions they pose. The duty-based approach is especially concerned with the three main duties of justice, respect and of doing no harm, which sometimes include the fourth duty, to benefit.

Box 1.7   Summary of three ethical frameworks and questions they pose

Duties (deontology)

- Justice – are the aims and methods right and fair?
- Are possible benefits and burdens of research shared fairly?
- Respect for autonomy – do researchers treat participants as they themselves would like to be treated?
- Do no harm – might the research be harmful or useless?

Rights

- Do the researchers respect participants' rights to:
  - o what is so far known to be the best available treatment, care or resources?
  - o protection from harm, neglect and discrimination?
  - o self-determination, such as to give informed consent or refusal?
  - o non-interference and to research that is not too intrusive or restrictive?

Harm–benefit (utilitarianism)

- How can researchers reduce or prevent harm and increase the chance of benefit from their work?

(Continued)

(Continued)

- How do they decide which are the best outcomes to aim for?
- Whose interests do they put first, the child's, the parents', or the interests of the research, or of society?

Might there be harms in not doing the research, or in not involving children but instead listening only to adults?

Box 1.8 gives a hypothetical example of how the three frameworks apply to research about an extra support programme for young people. It shows how there are disagreements within, as well as between, the frameworks.

Box 1.8   Applying the frameworks of duties, rights or harm–benefit

An extra support programme is planned for young people in the community who are dependent on drugs, are self-harming and sometimes talk about committing suicide. The programme staff differ strongly in their views about whether to offer the new scheme. (The staff also argued about the best methods for testing the scheme according to the three frameworks but we have not listed that debate here.)
   The different *duty-based* replies might be:

- We must provide the new extra-support scheme at once and fairly to every young person, and keep careful research records.
- We must protect everyone from an untested scheme, and not simply test them in order to benefit others.
- We must respect the young people by informing them and letting them decide whether to join the research scheme.
- How can we choose fairly which people to offer the limited scheme to?

The *rights-based* replies might include:

- Everyone has a right to be in the scheme.
- Everyone has the right to be protected from the scheme.
- Everyone has the right to make an informed decision about whether to join the scheme.

The *harm–benefit* replies might include:

- We must decide whether the scheme is worthwhile by weighing the possible benefits to each young person against possible harms of the scheme, or the harms of not being in the scheme.

- We should weigh the risks and hoped-for benefits to young people in the pilot scheme against those to many future young people, who might join the scheme if it works well, or be protected from joining if it does not work.
- The risk–benefit balance is so uncertain, only the young people can decide.

Limitations and advantages of the three frameworks

(1) Ethics does not provide clear, agreed solutions. Its main use is as a method for exploring dilemmas in order to understand them more clearly and deeply. Each person tends to favour one or more frameworks, and it helps to understand where they are coming from, to save time by stopping people from going round in circles and talking at cross purposes.

(2) There is often disagreement within and between the frameworks, and debate about which framework is best. Rights and duties tend to refer back to ancient rules, and the aim to do 'what is right' might sometimes seem harsh or unfair. Harm–benefit analysis looks forwards to probable outcomes of the decision. The aim is to do 'what seems best', though this may excuse harm to small groups for the benefit of larger groups.

(3) Discussions about ethics tend to be rather bare and abstract, and to ignore real complex details in each case.

(4) New ways of thinking need to be developed in the ethics of research with children. Traditional ethics rightly stresses the importance of non-interference, and of avoiding deliberate harm, but little is said of the harms of over-protecting children by silencing and excluding them from research.

(5) The rights of different groups can conflict, such as between: (a) children (or other people) who use services or take part in research; (b) parents and other adults providing care, public services, or research; and (c) the public who pays for these services (see Chapter 4).

In research about conflicting interests, and unequally held power and resources, there is no central neutral or impartial ground. It is therefore useful for researchers to examine where their loyalties lie, and to question and try to justify their position.

Despite their limitations, the three frameworks offer useful ways of thinking about potential problems in social research, and of preventing or mitigating the effects of the problems. The frameworks are widely understood, and are based on common concepts in daily use. Even young children are keen to talk about justice, rights and being kind and fair (Gordon-Smith, 2009), although they may not directly use rights language. Yet the frameworks can also confuse detailed ethical assessments, when they seem to conflict or when it is not always clear how they can be put into practice.

Can ethics standards work in every country?

One view is that cultures vary so much that each culture has its own ethics. Certainly, ethical research has to be sensitive to local concerns, values and customs, and adapt to them. Yet how far should ethical standards vary between countries, for example, informing children and adults honestly, asking for their consent, and respecting their refusal? Although cultures vary, each one is not purely different from all other cultures, when so many influences flow between them. There are also too many varied views and disagreements within each culture to allow easy generalisations about what 'everyone in this place' believes.

Lukes (2008) argues that among all the many varied values there are constant principles and rights that matter in every society: justice, respect, solidarity, honesty, and these therefore form the core principles in this book. People vary in how and why they express and experience respect, and the related feelings of dignity or humiliation, confidence or powerlessness, being valued or being exploited or deceived. However, these experiences still matter to everyone, and when researchers ask participants to help them, they have a duty to honour these principles.

Uncertainty – the basis of ethical research

We noted in the introduction that research involves asking and trying to answer hard, searching questions. Researchers therefore have to start from uncertainty when they test interventions, explore users' views, or investigate old and new practices when no one yet really knows the answers. How do people, who have worked with children for years, step back and begin to ask:

- Is my work really effective?
- Should I use better methods and how do I know which ones are better?
- Do I have the courage to doubt my own certainties?
- Is it fair to worry the children and adults I work with, with these troubling questions?
- How will that affect the confidence that my service users need to have in me and as a practitioner I need to have in myself and my work?
- Surely being a professional means knowing the answers, not asking these questions? (See Box 1.9)

Box 1.9   Risking and learning from uncertainty

A reception teacher (Brooker, 2002) decided to research why five-year-old children, whose families came from Bangladesh, did less well at her English inner-city school than white, working-class children. She found how small

---

differences in family life, in parenting practices, views on childhood, beliefs about work and play, and their stress and illness levels made big differences to the children's adaptations to school and their success or failure in their early days there.

Perhaps most important, and certainly more difficult, she looked critically at her own profession. She saw how structures in schools, teachers' good intentions, and institutionalised racism led some children to become disaffected and to learn how to fail.

Teachers' aims to allow all children to follow their own interests and develop their own learning are inclusive in theory, but Western in practice. Many rules are not taught, but must be learned and worked out by the children. This is easier for children living in Western homes and culture than for others, who have many more boundaries to cross but are least likely to ask for help.

The study closes by urging teachers:

- to be alert to children's own ways of seeing and understanding and representing the world to themselves;
- to relinquish and transfer some of the power to make decisions about curriculum and pedagogy to parents and children;
- and so to create more equal, co-operative and rewarding relationships with them.

To raise these critical questions can involve a change of emotions and values as well as a change of mind. It can make professionals feel anxious and vulnerable while they develop new attitudes towards their own knowledge and status, and towards their service users' own views. Researchers have to accept that 'good practice' is informed by research and evaluation that take account of service users' views. Ethical research depends on professional and also public education about uncertainty, as well as on the courage honestly to admit uncertainty.

When traditional frameworks of duties, rights and harm–benefit are applied to research designs, the ethical questions raised by research become clearer. Yet, there are further important though often hidden questions, as later chapters review.

Summary of questions

- What is the research for?
  - to learn more about children's and young people's views, experiences or abilities?
  - to develop or evaluate a service or product?
  - some other positive purpose?

- Whose interests is the research designed to serve?
- If the research findings are meant to benefit certain children, who are they and how might they benefit?
- What questions are the research intended to answer?
- Why are the questions worth investigating?
- Has earlier research answered these questions?
- If so, why are the questions being re-examined?
- How are the chosen methods best suited to the research purpose?

Two

Assessing harms and benefits

This chapter reviews the ways of assessing risks, harms, costs and benefits in social research. Assessments are important for two reasons. During planning, they enable researchers, reviewers and funders to decide whether the research is worth doing at all, or could be made less risky. And later on, these assessments help each potential participant to make an informed personal decision. Informed consent is the legal means of transferring responsibility for risk-taking from the researcher to the participant, and consent is only 'informed' if the risks are explained and understood. It is useful to think about harm–benefit during the early stages of planning research, when it is still possible to redesign the study fairly easily to reduce risks.

Harms

When researchers and review committees consider ethical aspects of a research project, they can help to protect children from the abuses of over-research. Over-research might mean too many children being in a study, or too many interventions, too much intrusion or too many repeated studies on the same questions. There are also problems of under-research. These include studies that miss out vital questions, or have such a low budget and short timescale, or to few children, that they cannot be finished or reported adequately. A very large and important area of under-research is the many services that are not evaluated at all, and which may therefore carry on unchecked, being useless or even harmful. For example, ways of caring for children, especially disabled children, which were once approved are now viewed much more critically through the eyes of the children affected. Some evaluations have collected only adults' views and miss children's possibly very different views. And there are numerous crucial areas where no one has yet systematically investigated children's views and experiences.

'Harm' is often invisible and elusive, complicated by different estimations, different viewpoints – researchers', children's or carers' – and differences between short- and longer-term outcomes. Medical research can seriously and immediately harm people, so that the need there for ethical controls seems obvious. In contrast, many social researchers see their work to be largely benign, or at least harmless. And yet social researchers can intrude into people's lives, and cause them great distress and embarrassment during the research. Afterwards, reports in books, journals and in news media may also cause great and long-term harm to individuals who are identified, and also potentially to large groups if, for example, the researchers recommend policies that are actually ineffective and damaging.

Benefits

Much social research, through its reports and recommendations, is intended to improve conditions for young people. Reports also help to increase information about children's own views and experiences that can change policies and public and professional opinion in a whole range of services in countries across the world (Percy-Smith and Thomas, 2010). Yet many researchers point out that most reports based upon children's views continue to be ignored (Willow et al., 2004). Research alone seldom brings real benefits without time and effort being spent on disseminating and implementing the findings (see Chapters 9 and 10). This is where 'insiders' such as youth workers, who are evaluating their own work, or people campaigning to keep a service open, tend to have an advantage over 'outsiders', who tend to lose contact after a research study.

Some researchers report direct benefits during research, such as when interviewees enjoy having a willing listener. Yet this is not the purpose of research studies, when the main aim is to collect data. Talking, in itself, may not feel like a benefit to the person concerned, especially if nothing happens after the research to address their problems. Another supposed benefit is in the friendly relationship between the researcher and the child participant. Since research is often about disadvantaged children, is fleeting friendliness really helpful? How do children who may already feel rejected or betrayed react when the friendly researcher departs with the data and makes no further contact? Who benefits in the long term?

We have raised these 'real world' problems to show the importance of researchers being honest and fair about their aims and interests, and about the likely benefits resulting from the research. Researchers should explain, for example, when children describe changes they would like to see, that these cannot be promised and may not happen. When the time and budget are too limited for follow up contact, researchers may need to explain this. Funds permitting, the research team could work with a support person, perhaps someone known to the children and young people, to give this ongoing contact. After sensitive interviews, some researchers phone the person a week later to see if they would like to talk further or to meet someone who will give support. There is the risk that people who feel hurt by the research will not want this kind of contact.

Risk, cost, harm and benefit assessments

To prevent harmful or inefficient research, risk–benefit assessments can be made at three levels:

- by the researchers;
- by ethics, funding and scientific review committees and advisers;
- by the potential participants and their carers.

All these groups need to have answers to the questions in Box 2.1.

Box 2.1   Information needed to decide on the risks and benefits of a study

- What questions or problems will the research deal with?
- Why do these matter?
- How common and how serious is the problem or lack of the knowledge being researched?
- If methods are being tested or compared: Are they new and/or already widely used? How do they differ from accepted methods? What alternative methods are there?
- Is the need to involve children justified?
- Exactly what will participants be asked to do?
- What direct risks might there be to them? (intrusion, distress or embarrassment, loss of the standard teaching or care methods, risks of new or untested methods)?
- How likely and severe might any risks be?
- How are risks reduced, such as by: Making police checks on researchers before they can meet children? Rehearsing with children ways to say 'no' when they do not want to reply? Assuring them that this will be respected, and they will not be questioned about why they refuse? Ensuring that children who feel worried or upset about the research can talk to someone about it afterwards if they wish? It can be useful to try to find out gently why young people want to refuse. Does the research seem boring or irrelevant? Could it be improved with their help?
- How can children contact the researcher if they want to make enquiries or complaints?
- What are the systems to review complaints, and then possibly change the research plans?

(Continued)

(Continued)

- How much of the participants' time will be needed for the research?
- What payments, fares and other expenses, such as escorts' fares or taxi fares for disabled people, or parents' childcare costs, are covered by the research? How can costs be reclaimed and how soon are they repaid? People often need to be repaid at once.
- How will the research findings be used?
- What are the planned outcomes, such as a report, or a film, or a product?
- Who are they designed for?
- What effects might they have?
- Which individuals or groups stand to benefit from the research outcomes in future? Roughly how many people? Do the research participants belong to that group? Might the findings benefit them, directly or indirectly?
- If there are any hoped-for 'benefits' from the research what might they be?

Confusion in risk–benefit assessments

Benefits

Risk–benefit analysis is often misunderstood. It is sometimes summarised in this way: 'You weigh up the benefits the research will bring, and the risks, and if the benefits are greater than the risks, then it is all right to do the research.' Yet analysis is not that simple, for the following reasons.

- How is benefit defined? Adults' views on 'benefit' may differ from children's.
- Some benefits or harms may only be known long after the services and research about them have ended, for example, potential later effects of parenting programmes or medicines for childhood behaviour problems.
- There may be short-term but no long-term advantages.
- It may be impossible to show that any benefits result from the new programme, when many other factors are involved.
- Benefits from social interventions can be hard to define and assess precisely, such as in actual changes in attitudes or behaviours.
- Chance associations may be mistaken for causes of benefits.

Risks

'Risk' is a vague word, to cover *possible* and definite harms, costs and inconvenience. In contrast 'benefits' implies that there will be definite good. So 'risk–benefit' is a loaded term. 'Risks and hoped-for benefits' is a more balanced phrase, and is more honest about the uncertainty underlying all research.

The risk to a few participants may be balanced against hoped-for benefit to countless young people in future, for example, in research on methods of mathematics teaching or of support during foster care. However, the danger here is that researchers can then justify any research by claiming huge hoped-for benefits. They need to be clear whether they are considering risk and benefit to each research participant, or are using the much looser equation of risk to the participant and hoped-for later benefits to society. *Helsinki* (WMA, 2009) and other codes repeat that the researcher's first concern must be the effects on the individual research subject, though some guidance is vague about individual risks versus collective benefit (see also Boxes 1.7 and 1.8).

Probability

How likely is the harm to occur? Risk probability can partly be counted. The risk of being knocked over if you cross a road can be worked out from the current average rates. However, it is a very vague measure; so much depends on the type of person and road and injury. The traffic accident injury rate may then be counted as an 'everyday risk' in the dubious belief that people will accept similar levels of risk in research as 'minimal'.

Severity

How serious might the harm be? Risk severity cannot really be measured because so much depends on each person's values. For one child, it might be fine to talk on television about crime in her area. Another child might be terrified for months afterwards about being picked on and attacked by local criminals. Probability and severity are often discussed as if they are the same thing, whereas they are very different.

Risk of distress or humiliation

Risks in social research and consultation include distress and anxiety, embarrassment and loss of self-esteem. If researchers are to explain risks, and how probable and severe these might be, they need to listen to children's views on which risks worry them most; some risks might not occur to researchers. A simple question, such as asking children if they would like to take part in a research study in groups or pairs with their friends, could upset children who feel they have no friends. A 'warm up' question, 'Who do you live with?' can distress children if there has been a recent death or separation in the family.

Other usual harms in social research and consultations, such as inconvenience, time lost, intrusion and mental discomfort, may seem slight. However, these could be very serious to the person concerned. People can feel wronged by research, if they feel they have been treated as objects, deceived or humiliated, or that their values or privacy have been disregarded, or their views were misreported. Research ethics is intended to help researchers to plan ahead and prevent such problems (Allen, 2005; Danby and Farrell, 2005; Farrell, 2005; Morrow, 2005; Cashmore, 2006).

Box 2.2 Distress during interviews

Ruth Evans, University of Reading UK, and Elsbeth Robson, University of Malawi, Africa and Brunel University, UK

We interviewed young people caring for family members with HIV/AIDS and recently orphaned children in Zimbabwe, Tanzania and the UK. Questions about their caring responsibilities, parental illness and the death of some parents sometimes led to tears and emotional upset. We tried to be sensitive to signs of distress and to offer a break, or to defer or end the interview. We found that talking about photographs children had taken, their drawings or a life story book they had completed, sometimes helpfully diverted attention from distressing topics. Researchers need to balance the potential harm (emotional distress and tearfulness) that may be caused by interviews against the potential benefits of the research for children, both individually and collectively, of sharing feelings, perhaps gaining confidence and relief by talking about memories, and contributing to the research, which might in future benefit other young carers. Researchers need to provide quiet private interview settings, and to see whether children may wish to have emotional support from other project workers wherever possible (Evans and Becker, 2009; Robson, 2001).

The research in Tanzania and the UK was led by Ruth Evans and Saul Becker, University of Nottingham and funded by the ESRC (Grant number RES-000–22–1732-A). Elizabeth Robson led the research in Zimbabwe, funded by the Royal Geographical Society with the Institute of Geographers.

From very many reports on child abuse research, we cite here one example, because it provides such a detailed analysis of ethical problems with practical ways to address the problems.

Box 2.3 Child abuse research

Neerosh Mudaly and Chris Goddard (2009), Monash University, Australia

Nine young people aged 9–18-years-old, who had been abused were interviewed. Among useful precautions, the researchers carefully reviewed the ethical

---

arguments for and against and the potential problems of conducting inter-views about abuse. We selected young people who had received therapy, which was also offered during the research. We did not ask directly about abuse, leav-ing each person to decide how much to say, while we were careful not to appear as if we were unable or willing to hear painful accounts. We involved primary carers and used 'child-centred' research methods, counselling techniques, and requests for informed consent.

We believed that while some children experienced 'interview-engendered distress' (Amaya-Jackson et al., 2000) they were not re-traumatised. Our papers conclude with lessons learned about when it is appropriate to involve children who have been abused and what could have been done differently (Mudaly and Goddard, 2006, 2008).

Welfare

'Until the lions have their own historians, history will always be written by the hunter' (South African proverb, in Lolichen, 2006). The child harm and abuse literature tends to contrast children's 'welfare' rights, meaning protection, with their participation right and need to be heard. This can rather skew decisions against research with children and deter researchers (Beale and Hillege, 2004; Skelton, 2008; Powell and Smith, 2009), RECs and gatekeepers (Carroll-Lind et al., 2006), if 'welfare' is identified wholly with protection. The processes and potential outcomes and benefits of 'participation', the right to protest, to have one's views taken seriously, to influence future policy and practice, potentially to set wrongs right and prevent future wrongs, are surely all part of welfare (Lolichen, 2006). To contrast welfare with participation could imply that participation can only be risky and non-beneficial to the child. The contrast could also imply that adults can ensure children's welfare without necessarily hearing and being guided by children's views, whereas abuse occurs when children are silenced, and is evi-dence that adults are not always benign. To replace 'protection' with 'welfare' partially conceals adults' active and at time negative controls. Reviews of the ethics in child abuse research would be clearer if the terms 'protection', 'welfare', 'participation', 'harms' and 'benefits' were used more precisely.

Summary of questions

- What contributions are children asked to make to the research? such as activities or responses to be tested, observed or recorded?
- Might there be risks or costs? Time, inconvenience, embarrassment, intrusion of privacy, sense of failure or coercion, fear of admitting anxiety?
- Might there be benefits for children who take part in the research? satisfaction, increased confidence or knowledge, time to talk to an attentive listener?

- Are there risks and costs if the research is not carried out?
- How can the researchers promote possible benefits of their work, and prevent or reduce any risks?
- How will they respond to children who wish to refuse or withdraw, or who become distressed?
- Are the research methods being tested with a pilot group?

Three

Respect for rights: privacy and confidentiality

Privacy is a vital ethical concern although it has not always been respected in research with adults or children. This chapter reviews children's rights to:

- privacy (avoiding undue intrusion into their personal affairs); and
- confidentiality (concealing their identity and sometimes other details when reporting them).

The first section reviews legal rights, and reports an Australian court case on confidentiality. We will then compare opt-in and opt-out access methods, give a detailed check list on respecting privacy, and look at the Data Protection Act 1998, recommending good practice on ways to respect confidentiality. This chapter also considers questions about privacy raised by intimacy between strangers during research interviews, and in research on the Internet. The final section asks whether duties, rights and utilities (see also Box 1.6) need to be complemented with greater concern about complicated relationships, detailed practices and emotions in research.

Legal rights to confidentiality

Children have many of the same rights to confidentiality that adults have. For example, competent children can ask and expect their doctors not to inform anyone else about their case (Brazier and Cave, 2007: 406–7). Children have some extra rights, such as their names not being published in the media if they are involved in the family law courts in England (although their rights to anonymity in the criminal courts have been reduced). No one has an absolute right to confidentiality in research and, in rare cases, confidentiality may be broken, if it is thought that someone is in serious danger. If so, the researcher should first encourage the person who knows about the danger to talk to adults who could help, or otherwise to agree that the researcher should talk to them. 'Guarantees of confidentiality and anonymity given to research participants must be honoured, unless there are clear and overriding reasons to do otherwise, for example in relation to the abuse of children' (BSA, 2002). The BSA guidelines also state: 'Research involving children requires particular care … Specialist advice and expertise should be sought where relevant', though without saying where these should be sought.

There are two key ethical questions relating to confidentiality:

- If it seems necessary to breach confidentiality, is this first clearly discussed with research participants?
- Should participants be warned before they consent about the limits of confidentiality?

It is often said that researchers cannot promise confidentiality to children, in case children describe abuse or other information that must be reported to, and is perhaps demanded by, the courts. However, a decision of the Family Court of Australia, which respects children's confidentiality, has important influence on law in over 50 British Commonwealth countries (Box 3.1). See also Williamson et al. (2005), who discuss questions of confidentiality relating to child protection, and Kendrick et al. (2008), who discuss questions of privacy and confidentiality in research with children and young people in residential care.

Box 3.1   Research and promises of confidentiality to children: a legal challenge

Research conducted with children under express promises of confidentiality may be protected from subpoena (a court order to provide evidence, the research data). The case of T v L (unreported, 12 October 2001) involved research about children's participation in making decisions about residence and contact following their parents' separation. The researchers took great care to interview parents and children, who were contacted through the Family Court, only after legal proceedings were thought to be completed, and with parents' express and explicit undertakings that confidentiality of all data would be respected, and that no further legal proceedings were contemplated and no subpoenas would be sought. However, one father, Mr T, later issued a subpoena (application through the courts) to have copies of the notes and tapes of his children's interviews. The judge, Collier J, struck down the subpoena on three independent and each vitally important grounds: public policy, and assuring researchers and participants that confidentiality in research is respected by the courts; precedence from a former case and holding Mr T to his earlier agreement that his children's interviews would be confidential; relevance, and lack of definite and legitimate purpose on Mr T's part for wanting to see the data.

(Example contributed by the researchers of this case, Patrick Parkinson and Judy Cashmore, University of Sydney.)

Opt-in or opt-out access

Opt-in research can be more respectful of privacy than opt-out. With opt-in, researchers send letters, often by a third person, inviting people to telephone or return cards if they want to take part in the research or to receive more details. Only then may the researchers know the details about those who reply. However, this can create barriers that make it harder for researchers to contact certain groups, especially disadvantaged and excluded ones, and to include their views. This can not only distort research findings, but also lead to further discrimination against the groups that may be most in need of research findings that explain and report their difficulties.

Opt-out research increases the numbers and range of participants by getting higher return rates, so that it can be more inclusive, realistic and even democratic. However, it can invade privacy. Imagine someone who has phoned or sent a letter saying that unless you cancel the visit, a researcher will call, and who then knocks on your door and will not leave unless you say firmly that you do not want to consent to take part in research – something you may find hard to do. Box 3.2 describes one solution to these problems, which readers may wish to debate.

Box 3.2   Opt in or opt out by seldom heard groups?

Ruth Marchant, Triangle

Opt-out research forms were sent to looked-after young people but did not reach them all. Those who did not return opt-out forms were contacted by researchers without their agreement. But opt-in methods can involve losing many people who might like to take part but who do not contact the researchers as requested. Their parents/carers may report that young people are not interested in joining a research study, their social workers may not pass information on to people with sensory, learning or language difficulties, worried that they are not competent to consent or refuse, even when researchers have made extra efforts – modifying participation requests and research methods, and involving translators/signers.

We usually achieve 98 per cent inclusion of children or families, whereas an earlier project involved only 10 per cent. Some recruitment methods discriminate against hard to recruit groups, whose views need to be heard and hardly ever are. To research with 30 families, we ask social services for, say, 90 names and addresses. Social Services then send families a letter saying that, unless they indicate otherwise, their details will be sent to the research team. We then select 30 names and social services do not know which 30 they are. We send an information pack and letter saying that unless the parents indicate otherwise, a researcher will ring the parent or child at home. A senior researcher will then ring the parents. They rarely refuse despite being traditionally 'hard to reach' families.

See http://www.howitis.org.uk on image vocabulary to help children to communicate on feelings, rights and safety, personal care and sexuality.

Practical respect

This section looks at respect in a range of methods and questions for readers to consider. In the use of records, for example, case notes, archives of longitudinal research and other data, when the people recorded are not approached directly, would they mind how their data are used and interpreted, particularly in secondary research? Should they be contacted and asked for their consent?

With questionnaires, how far is it right to ask questions that might offend or upset people? Do questionnaires and highly structured interviews omit topics, questions and optional replies that participants would consider vital, or that would help to make sense of their seemingly illogical replies or behaviour? Some young people, for instance, might give logical reasons for missing school.

Do the questions and approaches respect each age group, without belittling younger children?

Tape recordings, videos, photographs, drawings, maps and diaries raise extra questions about confidentiality. Who should have copyright and possession of originals, and should children's authorship be acknowledged or their names kept secret? (See also Box 7.3.)

Interviews range from highly structured question-and-answer sessions to informal conversations. As with group discussions and other group activities, do the researchers exert too much control, in ways that make the participants uneasy? Do children feel made to say more or less than they wish to? During semi-structured sessions, people can seem to have more control and choice in what they say. Yet these can also be more self-revealing sessions, which are widely open to being misinterpreted and misreported.

Here are some reminders about respect for privacy and confidentiality.

How and why have people been chosen? If their names are on confidential lists, such as 'at risk' registers, will researchers ensure that they do not see the lists? Only professionals with access to the list should select the names and approach the people. If the people agree, the researchers can then be informed, are the people told about the means of access to their names and why they were chosen?

Is everyone given a choice about whether they are tape-recorded or, if they prefer, are notes made instead?

How will the data – notes, audio or video tapes – be stored under the current Data Protection Act? (See below.) Are interviews held in a quiet private place (this can often be hard to arrange in homes and schools) and can interviewees choose if they wish anyone else to be present?

Are participants told that everything they say will remain confidential (private) and only be quoted when they cannot be identified?

Do the participants want this? Would they rather be named and acknowledged? If so, what is the best response?

Are they warned about limits to confidentiality if they mention serious risk of harm to themselves or to others?

In research that uses group discussions how is confidentiality for the people in the group, and the people they talk about, respected? This partly depends on the questions being asked – group discussions are not so useful as interviews for disclosing intimate information, but they can be very useful for eliciting shared views for example, about a local neighbourhood. 'Chatham House rules' can be explained clearly, even to young children. The rules mean that: 'After the group meeting, you can talk to other people about what we said. But please do not tell them the name of the person who said it, or the names of any people they were talking about.'

If other people than the research team will be given details about the research sessions, do the participants know and agree to these named other people being informed?

Who will see the research records, transcripts, notes, tapes or films? There is now more caution about using photographs of children, and about requesting children's and parents' consent before these are used.

Will research participants have a copy of any relevant letters to other people, such as if researchers write to teachers, psychologists or social workers about a child's responses to the researchers?

How will reports be published in ways that protect privacy (change of names and other details)?

Is consent to the use of data such as photographs or videos in public reports specifically requested from each person?

Do the research participants have any kind of editorial control, such as to ask for some comments they have made to be omitted from any reports, and to check for fairness and accuracy?

Are participants asked to agree to any follow up research, or secondary use of their data such as through data archiving? The ESRC, for example, wants data from all research to be archived, potentially for other researchers to use. When is it best to ask people for their extra consent to this? You do not want to overwhelm them with complicated requests before an interview, but is it good enough to ask them later in the study? Or is it better to ask them later, when they know much more about what they have said, and how they might like their data to be used or not used? (See Chapter 8 on consent to archiving.)

Privacy rights

Privacy is a very complex right. At one extreme, it can protect children to the extent of excluding them from research, with all the drawbacks and even dangers of silencing them, and ending their hope of influencing, through research reports, policies and practices that may be harming them. This denies their autonomy throughout the processes and outcomes of research. At the other extreme, privacy is the supreme original 17th-century autonomy right of adults to make their own decisions without interference.

Ethics emphasises respect, rights and equality, whereas most services for children emphasise protection over respect. The meaning of rights has expanded from the early rights of respect for autonomy, non-interference and privacy, to include *provision* rights to resources, such as education and health-care, and rights to *protection from harm*. However, provision and protection stretch the meaning of 'rights' from the original idea of non-interference, into active interference in the child's interests. While protection is important, over-protection can lead to children being treated as passive objects of concern, rather than as active moral agents in their own right. This can expose them to greater risks of being exploited and even abused by researchers. Explicit rights can help to clarify areas of conflict, and regulate relations between participants and researchers, as spelt out in the Data Protection Act 1998.

Data Protection Act 1998

Each fairly large research institution has an officer to advise on data protection, and to register research under the Act. People working on research projects in small agencies also need to check details of the Act and to register their projects. This includes keeping full details on:

- Purposes for holding the data.
- Sources of the data.
- Individuals and organisations to whom data are disclosed.
- The sorts of data you hold.
- Whether you hold particularly sensitive data such as ethnic origin.
- Whether you intend to transfer data abroad (see Box 3.3).

Box 3.3   Some key points from the Data Protection Act 1998

- Personal data are any data about a person (data subject) that can be used to identify that individual.
- Data must be obtained and processed fairly and lawfully.
- Individuals who supply data must be made fully aware of why they are asked to do so.
- Data must be held and used only for the specified, agreed purposes.
- Data must not be disclosed to any person or organisation other than ones mentioned to participants when the data are collected.
- Data should be adequate, relevant and not excessive to the purpose for which they are held.

- If there is no planned use for the data, it should not be kept.
- Data must be accurate and kept up to date.
- Personal data must not be held longer than is necessary. Data should be erased when there is no further use for it.

Individuals must be allowed access to any data held on them, including paper records (also under the Freedom of Information Act 1998). A print out must be produced within 40 days, including photocopies of all paper documents held on the individual. Institutions may be fined if they do not comply. This does not relate to research records, provided data are published in a purely anonymous statistical form and no data are disclosed that would help to identify an individual. If any sort of identification is published, then the data are no longer anonymous, and data subjects then have access rights. (In small qualitative studies, people may be quite easily identified, even when they are anonymous. It is wise to keep very careful, respectful records, in case the people concerned ever wish to see them.)

Good practice on confidentiality

- Take reasonable measures to ensure that unauthorised people cannot access the data in computer and paper records. If personal data are displayed on a screen, log out before leaving the office, even for a short while.
- During a research project, if you need to collect more or less or different data, or to disclose data to different people, you must alter your registration records.
- Take extra care with personal data defined as sensitive under the Act, such as about racial/ethnic origins, political opinions, religious beliefs, physical and mental health, sexual orientation or habits, and criminal convictions; and remember that participants may regard other details about themselves as highly sensitive.
- Only hold sensitive data if you have explained to the data subject why you are using the data, and the data subject has consented.
- All personal data must be handled with appropriate safeguards for the rights and freedoms of the data subject.
- If you save word processing documents with letters and other documents that contain names and addresses and other identifiable details, then you must register them. (It is better to anonymise all computer and other records, and to keep these separate from records of personal details.)

Respect for privacy rights at home

Parents/carers may want to join in young people's interviews at home. As 'guests' of the family, interviewers cannot easily request a private space for candid interviews, or use the privacy of the child's bedrooms for child protection reasons. Some children may prefer to be interviewed with their parents, at least for the first part of their session, and families' choices and interactions can provide very useful insights. Some parents help their children to give fuller replies. However, other parents may inhibit and irritate their children. If so, researchers may tactfully have to try to arrange a follow up in another setting.

Research with children in majority world countries: privacy and confidentiality

Beazley et al. note that 'social hierarchies and cultural mores may make it difficult to work with children away from the influence of adults' (2009: 364). Children and adults do not necessarily inhabit separate spaces in the same way as they do in minority world societies.

Box 3.4   'Privacy' in Ethiopia

Tatek Abebe (2009: 457), described his fieldwork in rural and urban Ethiopia and the difficulties of finding a space for interviews

... partly because finding appropriate places proved difficult and partly because of local conceptualisations of childhood, which regard children as having inferior social positions within households. In most cases, adults, parents and other children would simply come and join in, even if I was in the middle of conducting formal interviews with children. As someone who was born and raised in Ethiopia, I felt that asking people to give us 'privacy' was both a-cultural and an awkward way of handling the situation, especially since the physical space shared by members of the household is very small. Also, since researchers often speak to the 'heads' of households rather than to 'subordinate' members within them, focusing on children *per se* might have risked being seen as a threat to adult authority and power. What 'private views' do children have ... when they are seen more as members of the wider family collective and less as individual human beings?'

These examples can happen in any country. In the UK, for example, teachers often walk into rooms where 'private' research groups or interviews are being held. Some do not see a problem about staying to listen until the researcher politely asks them to leave. In homes, parents may want to listen, or think it is polite to stay, or have no other room to sit in. Researchers can feel awkward about concentrating for a whole interview on the child, when parents are present, because this is against the usual etiquette in most countries. They can find themselves looking and nodding and smiling at parents to avoid seeming rude.

Privacy is linked to time. At the first meeting or two, adults may feel they should be near and not leave the child alone with a stranger. In long-term research, it can feel much easier to leave well known researchers alone with children. During warm weather, researchers may be able to use gardens and playgrounds for semi-privacy.

Confidentiality or acknowledgement?

Sometimes, children want to be recognised for the research data they give and for their views and experiences, their drawings or maps. Yet if children are named, they may be identifiable. And if one child is identified, others in their group or school, who do not wish to be, may also become identifiable. These questions need to be discussed so that reasonably fair solutions may be agreed. Children can be asked to choose a research pseudonym for themselves. A study about premature babies, with the parents' permission, used the babies' second given name, although sadly one mother said she wanted her son to have an English research name in place of his Ghanian name, 'because otherwise people will not take his story seriously'.

In one study, when young people wanted their real names to be published, the researchers explained the reasons for using pseudonyms and that this was usually advised, especially in cases of sensitive data. Young people may want their names used now, but may not feel so pleased about being named in the future – and would be unable to change their minds. The researchers apologised for not doing what the young people preferred, and asked them to choose pseudonyms. The researchers also said that if anyone wanted to tell people they had been involved in the research, and share newsletters of the findings, that was, of course, fine – and up to them.

Intimacy between strangers: research interviews

Ethics pervades every step of research. For example, in interviews the aim is quickly to set up mutual respect, trust and rapport in order to obtain personal and sometimes intimate and distressing details. There is an odd balance between businesslike and friendly relations. This involves interviewers using sympathetic techniques:

- sitting at the same eye level, not too close or too distant, in a quiet, comfortable, private place;
- asking for permission to make notes or tape recordings;
- letting children hear their own voice on the tape if they wish;
- encouraging them by talking clearly, fairly slowly and not too loudly;
- looking and sounding interested;

- gently reflecting back by repeating points interviewees have made to affirm them;
- asking follow up questions and following leads from interviewees;
- checking verbally and through body language whether people are comfortable to continue talking.

Keeping eye contact is often advised. However, this can be intrusive and intimidating. Later we will describe very sensitive interviews when the researcher sat next to the child and they both concentrated on expressive craft work, which expanded children's ability to communicate and to have control over the pace and content of the interview (Winter, 2009).

Some children may agree to be interviewed but seem very unwilling or bored, shy or embarrassed during the interview. Some do open up with gentle prompting. If they do not, researchers could try further topics. If these do not improve matters, it is respectful to talk for a while and then end the interview positively and thank them without suggesting that the session was unsuccessful.

Some children like to have a copy of their transcript or tape but before offering these it is worth thinking about how confidential they might remain. The children may have said things about family members who might find the transcript and not be pleased.

Group sessions can be arranged like a meeting between friends, with chairs in a close circle, and simple requests such as 'please don't interrupt', 'listen to what each person says' and 'please talk clearly for the tape recorder'. Children should be able to feel free to have a break, pause, and say, 'I don't want to talk about that', or 'let's stop now'. Many researchers recognise that children may be more comfortable in pairs or groups, and often prefer to choose how they wish to take part.

These interactions can feel genuine to the researcher, although they do involve skilled techniques, and there is an imbalance between the data-giving by participants and the data control by researchers. However, rapport during interviews is complicated by the authority that adults hold over children. An assurance that 'you can tell me any time you want to stop' tends to deny powerful influences that may deter interviewees from saying they want to leave.

Skilled researchers are sensitive to children's reluctance, which children may be unwilling to express. People can be distressed by being asked questions, for example, about bullying, or disability or living in a family with HIV/AIDS. Even simple topics might very much distress people: pets, for instance, if their dog has just died and they are not ready to talk about it. Children should be assured from the start that they are free to withdraw at any stage, stop an interview or not answer a question, and this can be rehearsed before the interview. Researchers should be alert to signs of distress or reluctance. Road traffic style signs help children to show if they want to stop or withdraw (they can hold up the red disc), pause (the amber disc) or if they want to continue (the green disc). Genuine respect for young participants is honoured through all stages of the research, in efforts to collect, understand and present their views as fairly as possible.

Ethics and the Internet

New technologies bring people into very close contact across the world. Ethics guidelines urge caution (BSA, 2002) and researchers should take special care when researching via the Internet. Ethical standards for Internet research are not well developed yet, and eliciting informed consent, negotiating access agreements, assessing the boundaries between the public and the private, and ensuring the security of data transmissions all raise problems. People who do research online are advised to ensure that they know about ongoing debates on the ethics of Internet research, and to be careful about respecting the well-being and privacy of online research participants. Online direct consultations also raise these issues in this fast changing field.

Researchers on the Internet can meet with extra problems of privacy and confidentiality in the following ways when they:

- contact strangers who use the Internet to ask them to join a research study;
- post participants' responses online;
- run open or closed email lists or chatrooms;
- research participants' online messages, such as Bebo or Facebook, and find young people who seem unconcerned about privacy (Box 3.7);
- risk members breaking the confidence of a closed list and publicising sections;
- risk outsiders seeing or hacking into closed lists;
- risk members giving false details, when they do not belong to the selected group of young participants, and they may be adult voyeurs who threaten the privacy and safety of the selected group.

Some research teams are working hard on these challenging questions and on efforts to increase confidentiality, privacy, respect and security in online research, as well as to respect and publicise young people's own views, as the following examples show.

Safety and privacy in online research with young people who self-harm

Young people with psychological problems are often reluctant to seek help from health professionals, who can lack confidence in how to talk to them, particularly about self-harm. The SharpTalk Study explored how anonymous online contact could encourage young people and professionals to communicate and learn from one another. The experimental online discussion forum recruited young self-harmers (aged 16–25) and recently qualified mental health professionals (five years or less). It took nine months to secure ethical approval for this exceptionally challenging project (see Box 3.5). Safety of the researchers was also important, and they were supported by an independent

41

panel of experts on child protection, ethics and medical law. This example gives useful ideas on ways to gain REC approval for risky research.

Box 3.5   Safety in online research

SharpTalk: an experimental online forum for health professionals and young people who self harm
Dr Christabel Owens (PI) and Dr Siobhan Sharkey, Devon Partnership NHS Trust & Peninsula Medical School, Wonford House, Dryden Road, Exeter EX2 5AF

- Anonymity: It is easy to create a false online identity and particularly a false age. The REC therefore thought we should verify participants' real identity. Yet this would preclude anonymity, a crucial feature of online forums and one of the main reasons why young people seek advice and support via the internet. We believed that participants would feel safer if they were anonymous and we asked them to supply only a username, an e-mail address and a few demographic details. E-mail addresses were stored securely and seen by only one researcher. Participants were strongly advised not to post identifying information or photographs on the site, even though it was locked and only accessible to members.
- Consent: Likewise, printing, signing and mailing a consent form (the REC's preferred option) would have involved loss of anonymity. We took consent online but used a two-stage process, with a two-week window between stages, to ensure that participants had adequate time to consider whether or not to take part, and to require some commitment from them in order to proceed.
- Creating a safe and supportive community: Participants were required to abide by ground rules and a team of trained moderators monitored the site daily (till 2.00 a.m.) to check on compliance. Besides basic 'netiquette' (e.g. no abusive or offensive posts, no advertising), there were specific rules relating to self-harm, such as not sharing tips on how to self-harm or giving graphic details of methods. There was also guidance on labelling posts as potentially 'triggering' (i.e. likely to make someone feel like self-harming), suggestions of alternative things to do if you feel like self-harming (such as distractions and anger management techniques) and links to support sites. A dedicated 'crisis room' provided a container in which participants could seek help with particular issues and support each other in difficult times.
- Non-intervention: This was the most contentious issue by far. If a participant indicated online that they were about to make a suicide attempt, we could not alert any emergency services. We could find no feasible way of tracing the whereabouts of a participant in a crisis, and there was no guarantee that we would be able to intervene, even knowing the person's location. Instead, we drew

---

up a clear risk-management protocol for members of the team to follow in a crisis, including using the 'private messaging' facility, urging the individual to seek help and providing contact details of relevant agencies. Clinicians were on call throughout to provide advice.

Respecting local values

The next examples involve young people revealing their views in ways that could be judged or misunderstood by others. CHICAM (Children in Communication about Migration) was a Framework 5 European Union funded project in the UK, Sweden, the Netherlands, Germany, Italy and Greece, (2002–2005). Children in seven media production clubs in the six countries made videos about their lives, and shared them with all the clubs on the project Intranet, as a first stage to making them public. Among several ethical questions was international political safety.

- Even though the children had consented to their videos being put on the project Internet platform, were they able to assess the wider issues in relation to their own and their families' international, political and safety positions?
- Within these risks, how could the researchers maintain anonymity without resorting to pixilation which could seem to criminalise the children – particularly unsuitable for refugee and asylum seeking children?
- How do these children see the audiences for their videos, when some videos were quite personal and more suitable for family and friends than a wider audience?
- How do the children and the researchers assess the boundaries between public and private in the world of new communications technologies?

Box 3.6 Cultural values in cross national research and the internet

Liesbeth de Block, Institute of Education University of London, UK. http://www. chicam.org

During the CHICAM project, the Netherlands club made a video depicting the story in which St Nicolaas arrives from Spain with gifts for the children. This story is celebrated as a traditional national festival in December even more than Christmas. The children in the club were keen to explore this story that was new to them but which plays a central part in the life of their schools and Dutch peers. The researcher agreed that this would be useful. Unfortunately the story also portrays

(Continued)

43

(Continued)

a black slave boy who leads St Nicolaas' horse. The boy chosen to play the slave refused to do so. Some of the group and the researcher persuaded him to be a thief instead on the basis that this would be more 'fun'. The researcher also decided that all the players would wear black masks in an attempt to make things more 'equal'. Unfortunately the only masks available were in old minstrel style.

When researchers and children in the UK club saw the video they were taken aback at its racism and were not keen for it to be used on the intranet or on the public site. However, for the children who had made the video, it was significant in developing their peer connections and cultural understanding in their new country, an important theme in the research project. However, was it appropriate to put this video on the open project website? (de Block and Buckingham, 2007).

Box 3.7   Complications of privacy and respect in a study of social networking sites

Rebekah Willett, Institute of Education University of London, UK

We researched young people's interactions and self-presentations on social networking sites. After group interviews with school students aged 14–16, and with their permission, we visited their Bebo sites, and later interviewed them individually. We did not visit their private sites, only their public sites, but even these were clearly not meant for parents or teachers to see, and the young people told us they would find it strange if adults looked at them. Without permission to view all the sites of 'friends' of the interviewees, or comments left by friends, it was difficult to make sense of the interactions, when understanding the content depends on knowing the context. 'Daniella' called herself 'slut' online, and her tagline said, 'Hi Im Daniella And ii Like It <u>UpThe Bum.</u> Just Like Your Mum! And I <u>Suck Dick </u>For £5 =]'. An uninformed (adult) interpretation might conclude that this might mean Daniella was selling sex, but she explained to us that she was sharing jokes with a girl who had posted that tagline. Daniella retaliated by putting on her friend's site, 'I suck nipples for free but you have to ask nicely'. Daniella told us: 'I didn't mind because I know she was only joking. 'Cos I was on the phone to her at the same time. So she was going, like, ha ha, look what I've thrown on your Bebo … So I was like, no, look at your Bebo … it just started building up and got worse and worse.' They left their jokes for others to see, ending with the smiley face emoticon. When asked whether they trust others to read their comments in the way they intended, many interviewees indicated that only their friends read their sites, and would know when they are joking (Willett, 2009a, 2009b).

Researchers face challenges when reading online texts and images, and when considering not only research ethics about consent and confidentiality, but also the range and depth of data needed to understand online practices.

Summary of advantages and disadvantages of online consultation

Advantages:

- Children and young people often enjoy this method of communication and see it as relevant to their lives and interests.
- The approach can yield candid information about children's views and priorities.
- It works well with other methods of consulting, either to supplement other methods or to gather initial views at the planning stage.
- It can provide wide and cheap access to the views of children and young people.
- It can help to reduce social inequalities when disadvantaged children are involved, such as via their schools.

Disadvantages:

- Online consultation does not necessarily provide a representative group of children and young people, and some people may give several replies under different names.
- Many children and young people do not have access to computers.
- It is very hard to gauge anything about the characteristics of the children who are commenting – (some may be adults in disguise).
- If accessed through school, children's responses may be influenced by teachers.
- There can be extra problems of privacy and authentic participation detailed earlier.

Privacy and encouraging freely given responses in face-to-face contact

Can researchers use protective privacy to reduce their influences on children's responses? People's views are always partly influenced by time and place, what they know, and think, and how they feel at the time, as well as how they perceive the researchers and the questions. Besides these 'naturally occurring' contexts, how can researchers be supportive but also respectful of children's privacy and independence in order to avoid undue influence on their responses?

Box 3.8   Reducing influences on children

Esther Coren and Jemeela Hutchfield, Canterbury Christ Church University, UK

A qualitative study with children receiving therapy following sexual abuse collected children's views about interventions entered into an 'activity book'. Our aims were that the study should not harm participants, and that the results should benefit children receiving services in future. Therapists whom the children already knew explained the research to them, to avoid introducing another professional to the child. The research was conducted outside therapy sessions. It was explained to children that the research was entirely separate from therapy, and that participation would not affect therapy. Laminated samples of materials were used in introductions and explanations.

As the therapy and the practitioner were the subject of the evaluation, how could we ensure that children felt comfortable reflecting on their therapy experience honestly, without feeling implicit or explicit pressure from therapists? We decided that children would not show completed activity books to therapists unless they wanted to. Therapists were advised not to look at the children's activity books, and to answer their questions only by using the laminated samples. Children completed their books at home or, if necessary, in a quiet space at the project. Parents/carers were asked not to help (Coren et al., 2010; Hutchfield and Coren, forthcoming).

The next chapter will review benefits of using visual materials. However these can reveal children's identities. While images can bring new freedoms of creative expression to research, they can increase risks of participants being identified, and Box 3.9 suggests ways to protect children who use photographs.

Box 3.9   Photographs and substance use

Leeanne O'Hara, Institute of Child Care Research, Queen's University Belfast, Northern Ireland

An ethnographic study of young people aged 13–17 years, in Northern Ireland, examined the influence of neighbourhood, social and leisure contexts on their substance use and anti social behaviour. With rather conservative local groups who work powerfully and sometimes violently to deter substance use, protection of the young people's privacy and anonymity was even more vital. Each camera given to the participants was marked with the participant's research number and no other identifier. Their information sheet included guidelines for the use of cameras. Young people were asked to avoid taking photos of any faces including their own, and to ensure anonymity. If any faces were shown, full verbal consent for the photograph to be taken and used for research should be requested.

Does traditional ethics cover modern research experiences and relationships?

Box 1.7 outlined the duties, rights, and utilities or harms–benefits in traditional ethics. These tend to be impersonal approaches, not interested in emotions, and implying that research runs smoothly as long as it is well planned and managed. In practice, many problems and dilemmas arise throughout research projects, especially those on sensitive topics with children and other vulnerable groups. If social research ethics is to review complex details seriously, it has to take greater account of relationships, power and emotions (Boxes 3.10 and 3.11).

Box 3.10   Research relationships and power

- How do researchers' skills, in listening, talking and sharing knowledge and decisions with children, affect how they work with children as partners and learn from them?
- How do these skills affect the way researchers evaluate interventions, and their own work, and try to raise standards?
- How do researchers try to take account of power differences between adults and children, researchers and participants, service providers and users?
- How do they try to avoid the misuse of power, and to respect children's rights and interests?
- How do they learn the children's views on their own best interests?

Box 3.11   Emotions

- How do researchers try to be aware of their own feelings, their hopes for their research, or fear and anxiety about mistakes, or worry about lack of time and resources and about stress, uncertainty and failure?
- How do they try to learn from, and act on, these feelings?
- How do they respond to children's and adults' distress or anger?
- How do researchers celebrate positive aspects of their work?

The role of emotions in research is debated and researchers are increasingly reflecting on this (see Hallowell et al. [2005] for general examples; Ansell and Van Blerk [2005] on emotions and HIV/AIDS research in South Africa; Parsons [2005] and Robson [2001] both discuss research with children in Zimbabwe). Do emotions bring new insights or cloud judgement? Does emotion lead researchers to become over-involved? There are advantages when researchers identify emotionally with their participants, while still respecting and exploring personal differences.

In stressful and sensitive topics there is, perhaps, an ethical requirement that research teams provide support and debriefing for researchers. With researchers' agreement, this can be a valuable resource both to support individual researchers, and also to inform the research processes and findings by the insights gained through feelings.

Besides the rather inwards looking practicalities concerned with emotions as discussed in Boxes 3.10 and 3.11, ethical research also looks outwards to larger political concerns, considered in the next chapter.

Summary of questions

- How will the names of children be obtained, and will they be told about the source?
- Will children and parents be able to opt in to the research (such as by returning a card if they wish to volunteer)? Opt out methods (such as asking people to 'phone to cancel a visit) can be intrusive.
- Is it reasonable to send reminders, or can this seem coercive?
- Will research directly with individuals be conducted in a quiet, private place?
- How can privacy and confidentiality best be respected in online research?
- Can parents be present or absent as the child prefers?
- In rare cases, if researchers think that they must report a child's confidences, such as when they think someone is in danger, will they try to discuss this first with the child?
- Do they warn all children that this might happen?
- Will personal names be changed in records and in reports to hide the child's identity?
- What should researchers do if children prefer to be named in reports?
- Will the research records, notes, tapes, films or videos, be kept in lockable storage space?
- Who will have access to these records, and be able to identify the children? Using post codes instead of names does not protect anonymity.
- When significant extracts from interviews are quoted in reports, should researchers first check the quotation and commentary with the child or parent concerned?
- What should researchers do if respondents want the reports to be altered?
- Before researchers spend time alone with children, are their police records checked?
- Should research records be destroyed when a study is completed, as market and medical researchers are required to do?
- Is it acceptable to re-contact the same children and ask them to take part in another project?

Four

Designing research: selection and participation

Selecting the samples or groups you are to research is one of the first tasks in a project. New moves to include children work well if the ethics, methods, topics and outcomes of the research all reinforce one another, and are not contradictory. This chapter reviews the advantages and disadvantages of different framing and selection criteria. Traditional ethics tends to take a liberal position, as if everyone is equal, but this can side step politics, economics, social exclusion and inequalities, and the ethical problems they raise. Examples of social research with children from around the world show how research ethics can take a broader view of justice.

Framing the topics and extent of the research

Each research study has to exclude many issues in order to concentrate on specific questions and topics and to arrive at definite conclusions. Deciding how wide the research area is to be is like positioning a camera lens and choosing what will be inside and outside the frame. Social research has to take some account of the broad context that is both inside and outside the frame, deciding what is around or else central to the participants. There are no clear cut-off lines.

For example, research on school truants might simply record days absent. However, to understand truancy involves researching the truants' views and motives, and their experiences inside and outside school. This might lead to examining different school policies and budgets to explain variations between schools, and between factors such as family income, ethnicity, or health, or local employment opportunities. Box 4.1 shows how listening to young people brought vital findings into a study on exclusion..

Box 4.1 Extra exclusions

Although 17 per cent of students officially excluded from school are girls, they tend to be ignored. Girls feel that teachers set double standards, overlooking subtle

(Continued)

(Continued)

bullying among girls and girls' subdued depression, while intervening more to help boys. Help for girls is often poorly co-ordinated, especially when they are carers at home, are pregnant and have their own children, or are under pressure to work in escort agencies and prostitution. Many girls opt out and 'self-exclude', and unofficial and unrecorded exclusions are more likely to happen to girls than to boys. In vital ways, girls suffer extra problems that leave them even more unseen, unnoticed and excluded (Osler et al., 2002).

This kind of broader, more inclusive research can produce clearer analyses. It can also be more fair and ethical to take account of the wider context, rather than assuming that the problem lies wholly within the individual child or the parents. The broad or narrow framing of research relates to ethics and justice as well as to methods.

Advantages and disadvantages of exclusions criteria: research with children last?

Children are among the groups that have been most excluded from research. Medical ethics guidelines, in many ways rightly, say, 'Research which could equally well be done with adults should not be done with children' (RCPCH, 1992/2000:177). Most women are also often excluded from medical research in case they might be pregnant. Yet as a result, medicines are mainly tested on men aged 16–60 years, and little is known about the doses that children and women need and the reactions they might have to medicines. This medical example illustrates similar problems in other areas – education, play, social and voluntary services. When children's unique and valuable views are unknown for lack of research, because it is thought to be too risky to involve them, it is harder to ensure that the best opportunities and services are offered to them, or that harmful services are improved.

There are important protective reasons for excluding children from research:

- adults tend to have more experience, which can alert them to risks in research;
- adults have more confidence and independence to enable them to refuse or withdraw if they wish to;
- adults may have more resilience and be less likely to be hurt by the research;
- researchers are likely to take an adult's wish to refuse or to withdraw more seriously.

However, instead of emphasising children's supposed vulnerabilities, this book is concerned with how to design and promote ethical lower-risk research with, and for, children and young people.

Researchers often protectively exclude children who speak little English, or who have learning or speech difficulties. The research is therefore likely to produce incomplete and misleading findings. The opposite ethical approach is to make every process throughout the study as inclusive as possible. Then methods can reinforce the conclusions that inclusion is possible and can work very well. (See Box 4.2, and the Diversity and Difference Group project in Chapter 9.)

Box 4.2   Equal opportunities

The group Children in Scotland is committed to equal opportunities and believes that all children are of equal worth, whatever their ability, colour, ethnicity, gender, health, religion, sexual orientation or social class. These principles must be carried through into the design and conduct of research within the limits of available resources.

To promote inclusive practice, Children in Scotland say they will:

- Where possible, invite interested parties (including children and minority groups) to participate in defining the aims, design and key concepts of a study before it begins;
- Avoid the use of exclusionary language in research proposals;
- Within the limits of resources adapt or adopt particular techniques to ensure all those eligible can participate equally regardless of ability or literacy;
- Avoid condoning or perpetuating prejudice and stereotypes in the research that is proposed or conducted.

The guidance adds that recruitment must recognise diversity and use non-exclusionary methods http://www.childreninscotland.org.uk

---

Some disadvantaged groups, such as families with multiple problems, risk being over-included if they are asked to take part in many studies. Alternatively, they may be among the least consulted people, and the least involved in planning research. This is another area in which ethics committee review (Chapter 6) can help, to ensure that the benefits and burdens of research are fairly shared. That means that no groups are over-researched, and people who helped with the research can benefit, when possible, from any useful outcomes such as better medicines or teaching methods.

Combining respect, inclusion and protection

Ethics involves finding a balance between unwanted extremes. An anonymous researcher who contributed to the first 1995 version of this book, working with young people in contact with social services, tried respectful opt-in access methods, through the local authority and carers, but found, as so often happens, this can exclude young people.

> I do worry that these ethics guidelines might be used to block young people's access to reputable researchers. In our study, young people had to sign a letter and return it to us if they wished to be involved. Some of them appeared to be deliberately diverted from taking part, because for example they were all taken out swimming when we visited. It is very difficult for those who are being looked after to voice their opinions in safe forums. One young man was so keen to attend that he walked three miles to the meetings on three occasions. Again and again, the young people told us how much they appreciated the chance to talk in the groups. They asked for more such groups to be set up around the country. I do worry that too tight ethical guidelines might be used to shut the door on what young people have to tell us. That would be a retrograde step.

When planning, reviewing and assessing research, relevant questions to be raised include:

(1) Is it clear why children and young people are involved in the research?
(2) Is it clear, if they are excluded from research about them, why this is so, and if they have been asked to consent to being discussed and reported about by adults?
(3) Are parents or carers encouraged to stay with children during research sessions, if the children wish this? Young children can be more scared about being left with strangers, than about research interventions.
(4) Are efforts made to speak to children separately, if they wish to or if they seem to be intimidated when carers are present, to help them to express independent views?

Does traditional ethics cover social exclusion?

Traditional ethics tends to see society as fair and equal, working well to benefit every social group. A more critical view recognises that different groups compete for power and resources. If social research ethics is to review inequalities and exclusions seriously, it has to take account of unequal and unjust social structures, beyond traditional views of duties and utilities. The next section reviews ways of overcoming language barriers.

Images and symbols

Visual images offer ways to combine respect, inclusion and protection (Emmison and Smith, 2000). Young children, whose first language is not that used by researchers, and children with speech and language difficulties may find it hard to respond to research questions. Their limited speech or writing, or their silence, may be taken as evidence that they have few or no views. Methods that combine art and craft work or photography can open up their responses and their intense participation in research. PowerPoint slides can literally be power points, when young children skilfully select and paste in photographs and drawings with short captions that powerfully convey their ideas, and this frees them from writing detailed replies, perhaps unwillingly and laboriously.

The next examples of using art and craft, image and symbol, are of young looked-after children in Northern Ireland (Box 4.3) and then of Latino young people in Utah (Box 4.4).

> The interviews were based on the ethics of respecting children as persons, and seriously believing their accounts. The method of our sitting next to each other concentrating on the craft work enabled the children: to express their views visually and in symbols as well as words; to control the pace and content of the interview, such as by saying 'pass the glue' when they wanted to deflect questions or pause until they were ready to reply; to avoid eye contact that they might feel was intrusive or domineering. It was easier for me to pause and wait, to follow the child's lead, and to conceal my reactions, such as when I felt shocked. (Winter, 2009, 2010)

Box 4.3 Respecting young looked-after children's rights

Karen Winter, Queen's University Belfast, Northern Ireland

Formal inquiries after children have died of neglect or abuse usually find that no one listened to the child. My research has developed a method of encouraging young children to express their views, so that adults can make more informed decisions about their care. I asked children to decorate shoe boxes with craft materials, on the outside showing what kind of person they were, on the inside expressing their wishes and feelings. The interviews were very revealing. 'Crystal' aged 5 seemed cheerful and confident on the outside of her box.

C: It says that I am happy and kind and I love visiting my friends
    [Later on, the inside of the box was sad]
C: My baby who died This is the baby's eyes and teeth and that is a wee hat and hair ...
KW: What would you say to your mother?
C: You's stop arguing 'cos the kids is trying and the kids is missing you.

With her agreement, I referred Chrystal for bereavement counselling.
Connor, aged 7, was also sad, but I respected his wish to listen to him but not to refer him for further help.

(Continued)

(Continued)

C: Me wishes is um, er, to keep people happy ... On this bit of card, er, write me the word 'sad' and I'm gonna glue it down in my box so no-one can see it ... One more not nice feeling and that is, er what's that word with 'm' [*pause*] miserable. Could you do that on card for me? [*Long pause while he makes a fence of sellotape and lollipop sticks*] ... I put a fence round my feelings; that's why I don't want no-one to see them.

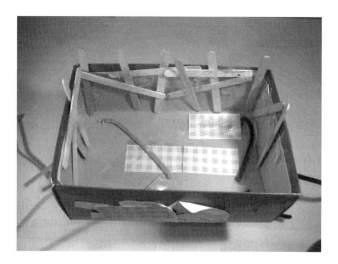

Box 4.4   Outburst comics: confidentiality and privacy in participation in transnational communities

A. Clotilde Houchon, PhD candidate with young comics researchers (2008–2009) Utah, USA

I collaborated with young people who were comics artists to create opportunities with them to communicate and take action related to their new lives and social relationships as immigrants. For example, 'Hafiz' in his comics research focused on the conflict he was experiencing with 'everyone', his parents, teachers and some of his friends. 'I received all F grades my first quarter in school...[my parents] don't speak English' and 'they think teachers are always right.' 'El Rey' was deeply upset by being seen as 'different, Latino and brown':

You know, when I was in school, there was no talk about what I wanted or needed. I'm Espana, so they automatically put me in ESL. Hell, they didn't even know that I was fluent in English. They [school counsellor] told me I'd never go to college. I was a bottom scrape, you know, the piece of trash a rat could eat, but I could draw! When I drew comics nobody was thinking, this guy is ESL. Drawing [comics] is a way to get out of this world, language don't matter in comics.

All these young people could talk freely through the visual codes in their multi-modal comics narratives by regulating point of view and perspective across language and culture in the presence of power. They analysed local and global social contexts, engaged in critical research collectively, and adapted to and transformed transnational social relations through a new surrealistic literacy practice. 'Comics inquiry', an imaged-based methodology rooted in a surrealism, was the composing space used to strip the ordinary of its normal significance and thus untangle the complexities of being where youth were and are simultaneously, as they created possible lives to grow into.

www.houchon.com/index.html

Beyond inclusion to participation: children and young people as researchers

What is participatory research?

There are not inherently 'participatory research methods', 'it depends how a method is used' (Beazley and Ennew, 2006: 192). 'Participatory' means that 'the people whose lives are being studied should be involved in defining the research questions and take an active part in both collecting and analysing the data' (Beazley and Ennew, 2006: 191). In reality, very little research is genuinely 'participatory' because the researchers usually set the main questions. Participatory rural appraisal (PRA) was developed over 20 years ago within international development studies, using visual techniques with non-literate rural communities. PRA has been useful 'in gathering information on the lives and views of people who lack power, and whose opinions are seldom sought' (Beazley and Ennew, 2006: 192). Genuinely participatory research 'is done by people in order to understand and challenge the problems they are facing' and it leads to action and change (Ennew and Plateau, 2004).

Ethics questions arise in participatory approaches for the following reasons:

- Often vulnerable, powerless groups are involved. Unless powerful groups also participate 'it is unlikely that the results can be used to develop practical policies to transform the lives of the poor and powerless' (Beazley and Ennew, 2006: 193) and so further oppression results.
- Occasionally the same groups are asked over and over again for their views, but very little change occurs, so their expectations may be raised and they may feel disillusioned by researchers' promises.

55

Children are increasingly involved as researchers. Concern about inequalities and inclusion has led researchers and others to work especially with (and not just for) disadvantaged children and young people to develop participatory approaches and techniques. Many reports and handbooks record peer research projects (for example, Smith et al., 2004; Christensen and James, 2008; Lolichen, 2007; Robson et al., 2009; and a study of looked after young people leaving care by peer researchers NLCAS, www.leavingcare.org.uk).

Box 4.5   Studies organised by young researchers from start to finish

Seven British children aged 9–10 years attended ten weekly research club sessions at school. They learned how to do research, then chose their topics and conducted their own research. Their reports set out their questions, methods, findings, discussion, and conclusions ending with a section 'if we could do this project over again we would ...' One report begins, for example:

> We were interested in how parents' jobs affect their children and wondered how children are affected by the kind of hours parents work and the sorts of moods they come home in, for instance if they come home very tired or angry or if they come home happy and bouncy. How does this affect the quality of relationships in the family? We also wondered how many parents worked and how long their hours were. We wanted to investigate this from children's viewpoints, not adults'. The research question we decided on was: 'how are children affected by the nature of their parents' work?' We predicted that most children would prefer their parents to work shorter hours and be able to come to watch them in more school events. What we found out surprised us.

The reports show how highly competent young researchers can be (Kellett et al., 2004).

In Kenya, children with HIV/AIDS were involved in researching, planning, implementing, monitoring and evaluating services for themselves and their peers. The ethical participatory methods helped to make services more effective, guided by UNCRC principles. The project workers reported that the children needed little training apart from information about the processes and purposes of the projects. The main training, they said, was for adults to help them to overcome their misunderstandings and mistrust of children, and to learn to work with them more equally (van Beers, 2002).

However, participatory approaches involve the same challenges and problems that other research has, especially when trained and paid researchers work alongside untrained and unpaid ones. Time and care are needed to train and support the researchers. There may be power, age, ability, ethnic and gender inequalities between the children and young people involved, as well as between them and the adults. Participatory and emancipatory research seldom achieves practical outcomes unless these are planned and worked for throughout the whole project (Davis and Hogan, 2003b). Manfred Liebel, Tom Cockburn and other authors in Antonella Invernizzi's and Jane William's (2008) book *Children and Citizenship* discuss problems with participation in research and innovative projects in detail.

Children and young people are themselves well aware of inequalities, as the girls who discussed whether there was a new local youth forum (Morrow, 2001) showed:

Gemma:	No-one knows about it, if there is one.
Tamisha:	I think there should be one, but …
Miranda (interrupting):	But they'd choose the people who do all the best in school and everything, and they're not average people, are they?

During research with disadvantaged groups, they do not want to be described with stigmatising terms such as 'socially excluded' or 'poor' and from their own view point they are not 'hard to reach' (Curtis et al., 2004; Sime, 2008). In some ways during participatory projects, the risks of exploiting children increase, and care is needed to avoid unethical pressures on both individuals and groups. The reports noted above include many practical ideas about working with young people on their own terms, and using young advisory groups to help to prevent and deal with problems.

It is also vital to remind children and adults that, in itself, research does not bring changes. Children and young people are eager to know what will change as a result of their research or consultation. The more they have invested, the greater their disappointment and perhaps disillusion could be if nothing is achieved.

Authorities may simply ignore even high quality reports. Or the research may not provide strong enough evidence to support a cause that the project was designed to promote. Even if some people are convinced by the data, critics may not be. Much extra hard work is usually needed, for a long time after the research has been completed, if policymakers and practitioners are to learn about and accept the findings and, possibly, implement them (Melville and Urquhart, 2002; and see Chapters 9 and 10). And by then, the young people will be older and may have moved on before any effects can benefit them.

UN-related work with young people

One example of international influence achieved by young people is the peer-led research and international advocacy by children and young people.

Sam Dimmock, head of policy and public affairs at the Children's Rights Alliance for England explains their UN-related work. The UK government (2007) sent its regular report to the UN Committee on the Rights of the Child in Geneva, on progress in implementing the UNCRC in Britain. *Get Ready for Geneva* was the three year project of The Children's Rights Alliance for England (CRAE, 2008a) when children and young people aged under-18 produced their own report for the UN Committee, and their own advocacy to effect change in public policy.

Box 4.6   National and international advocacy

The 15 investigators (aged 10–16) were trained in social research ethics and in interview, focus group and survey methods. They were helped to design the research topics and questions, develop online national surveys, and carry out focus groups with disadvantaged children (including those in custody or at risk of offending, young refugees and asylum seekers, children with disabilities, young travellers, looked-after children and children living in poverty). CRAE staff wrote briefing papers on each group and ideas for probing questions for the young investigators to use.

Data collecting over six months involved 1708 children and young people; 1362 responded to online surveys on education, respect, freedom and civil rights, family and friends, crime, health, safety and play. There were also online debates on participation rights in schools, the impact of age discrimination on young people, freedom of association, the quality of family life, being a victim of crime, healthy food in schools, and whether children have enough free time. The investigators ran 48 focus groups with 346 of their peers around the country, yielding over 3000 pages of transcripts.

Videos of the focus groups, and follow-up evaluation forms with both participants and young investigators were useful for tracking the investigators' skills and learning, and for continually improving and developing CRAE's practice.

The young investigators decided to write two reports. A longer research report of the full analysis and findings was written by the Get Ready team with input from children (CRAE, 2008b). After basic training, 30 children analysed the online survey data and 14 of them wrote their shorter report and recommendations (CRAE, 2008a), which they presented directly to the UN Committee in June 2008.

The impact of the child-led children's rights investigation has been far-reaching. The UN Committee reflected many of the children's findings, and all 14 of their recommendations, in its *Concluding Observations on the UK* (CRAE, 2008d, 2009; UN, 2008; and see UNICEF website). Children from the Get Ready project have since used their research and advocacy skills to develop discrete campaigns on children's human rights and further research. The UK government has also supported children in disseminating and debating their findings, not only with their peers but also with government ministers and key officials through a series of meetings and conferences. At international level, the involvement of so many children and young people in all aspects of the CRAE report has encouraged the UN Committee to look seriously at how it engages children in human rights monitoring mechanisms and CRAE young people's dialogue with the UN Committee has continued.

Box 4.7   Agreed ethics standards

Central to CRAE's human rights research work with young people is CRAE's (2007) *Research Ethics Statement*. Stated standards include the following.

- All research methods must be tailored to the needs and capabilities of participants and piloted prior to data collection.
- It may not be appropriate to consult certain groups in certain circumstances.
- 'Peer-led' research involves support and training and is 'relevant and grounded' in child and young people-led work at all stages of research. CRAE staff always attend research interviews and carry out a prior risk assessment.
- There are detailed standards on voluntary informed consent to interviews, tape-recording and the use of artwork, with an emphasis on jargon-free age-appropriate language and UNCRC based research standards.
- Details on parental consent are covered thoroughly.
- Standards are also set for confidentiality, anonymity, data protection and reciprocity – reporting back, thanking and acknowledging participants and respecting co-auhorship,
- De-briefing, reflection with peers and learning through evaluation forms are encouraged.

There is always a named person at CRAE to respond to complaints guided by the CRAE *Working with Children and Young People Policy.*

Respecting young researchers' own qualities

When research ethics includes a broader social and political analysis, the rights, duties and harm–benefit frameworks can be enlarged to gain a richer understanding of the research topics, context, methods and the impact of research on children, as reviewed in following chapters.

Box 4.8   Respecting young researchers' own qualities

Felicity Shenton, Investing in Children, Durham, UK, www.iic-uk.org

Investing in Children has promoted the human rights of children and young people to participate in all matters that affect them, since the mid-1990s. This includes enabling them to carry out their own research, which aims to 'find out what people think' and then record and report their views (see Tisdall et al., 2009). We involve young people in research design, methodology, fieldwork, analysis and dissemination. We aim is to achieve tangible changes that are recognised by young researchers themselves. The process involves 'finding out what you need to know to be able to create the best argument for change'.

When supporting young researchers (Lolichen et al., 2007), IiC is careful not to train out of them the very qualities and approaches that make them so distinct and authentic young researchers. We aim not to 'adulterate' either the people or the processes by training them to adopt adult methods and methodologies and views of the world, and the skills adults have decided they need.

In reality young people do use questionnaires, focus groups, interviews, participant observation, mystery shopping, and other research methods, although they may not use those terms. But they also use other informal methods, in adult-free spaces, to generate research evidence. Using the 'talk to people and write things down' approach they have developed a significant body of rich research data that is purposeful and focused on action.

The resulting ethical dilemma, however, is that adults, academics, managers, practitioners, decision makers, may not take this research seriously or see it as 'proper research'. This does beg the question 'Who is this research for? And whose purpose or needs does it serve?' IiC therefore supports children and young people to challenge adult views, and also helps adults to listen and understand, and to esteem young people's research as real, verifiable, significant and valid, and as valuable as any other research evidence (Lolichen et al., 2007).

Investing in Children has achieved changes. These include:

- Young people being involved in the re-design of schools as part of the Building Schools for the Future Programme in County Durham.
- Changes to the treatment and care of children and young people on the oncology ward at Alder Hey Children's Hospital Liverpool.
- The development of a pledge for children and young people who are part of Darlo Care Crew, the Children in Care Council within Darlington Children's Trust.

- Changes to the waiting areas, appointments system, information and communication provided to children and young people working with the Child and Adolescent Mental Health Services.

Box 4.9   Ethnographic research with young people on AIDS orphans' survival strategies in Uganda

Kristen Cheney, the International Institute of Social Studies, The Hague, the Netherlands

To address ethics, power dynamics, and knowledge production in ethnographic research with children, I put together a team of five former child research participants, aged 18–20 years. Some were orphans themselves. A local NGO trained them in social research techniques and paired them with five focus groups of orphaned children 5–10 years old. In exchange for school fees, the young researchers spent nearly two years visiting with their focus group children at school and at home, recording their experiences, thoughts, and challenges.

I gave up much of my authority in order to privilege the children's and young people's knowledge; data collected acted as a stimulus for dialogue in six different young researcher workshops. Together, the research team looked for commonalities and anomalies in their findings, interpreted the data, and generated new data from their impressions and new research questions for the next phase of the research. The extended ethnographic inclusion of children yielded important insights into children's experiences of orphan-hood, such as how they understand and deal with disease and death. These results have the potential to inform policy for better services according to children's reported needs.

This participatory, collaborative design brought many other advantages: it furthered common understandings of orphans' experiences and drove the research agenda in new directions centred on children's concerns. Regular reflection with the research team also helped build collaborative relationships between the children and adults in the project as they learned more about their own survival strategies, each other, and their community. In this way, participatory ethnography actually becomes *transformative* of young people and their communities. By the end, young researchers who were saying they never 'had a heart' for young children before had taken a vested interest in mentoring the children in their focus groups. They also met local stakeholders, received training in marketable skills, and gained work experience. Young researchers and caregivers from the study now comprise the local committee for the Empower Campaign, an international NGO that provides employment to caretakers and improves educational opportunities for orphans and vulnerable children. They are also learning to do cooperative needs assessments for children from the study and to help identify other beneficiaries in the community (Cheney, 2007).

Summary of questions

- Why have the children concerned been selected to take part in the research?
- Do any of them belong to disadvantaged groups? If so, has allowance been made for any extra problems or anxieties they may have?
- Have some children been excluded because, for example, they have speech or learning difficulties?
- Can the exclusion be justified?
- If the research is about children, is it acceptable only to include adult subjects?
- Are the research findings intended to be representative or typical of a certain group of children?
- If so, have the children been sufficiently well selected to support these claims?
- Do the research design and the planned numbers of children allow for refusals and withdrawals? If too many drop out, the research is wasted and becomes unethical.

Five

Money matters: contracts, funding projects and paying participants

Chapters 1–4 have reviewed choices mainly made during the early research design stages before it is possible to apply for funds, although the potential budget might have influenced the study design very much. The early choices were about the aims, questions and methods, although choice-making often continues into later stages. This chapter questions the sources of research funds, problems with budgets and timing, and how contracts can protect ethical standards. It ends with considering the payment of children and young people for their contributions to research.

Planning, budgeting and research agendas

Much ethics guidance sets high standards, but says little about how the complicated and often messy day-to-day conduct of research can fit these standards. This chapter reviews some of the complicated ethical challenges posed by funding and budgets. Over the past few years money matters have come to have a much stronger hold over research, as is considered in this first section.

Increasingly, commercial and university researchers have to include high overhead costs in their budgets. This can mean that social researchers are less able to apply to the charitable trusts, which do not cover overheads (as of 2009) but which tend to fund the more innovative, exploratory and participative projects. Apart from commercially sponsored market research, which is the largest sector of research with children, most funds are now granted by government departments and agencies, who increasingly support large research studies, evaluations and systematic reviews, mainly about children's and young people's needs and problems, and how services deal with these.

The potential benefits of such research are an improved understanding of children's needs and of effective ways to help them, as well as to check which services are not working well, possibly in order to remove or change substandard services. There are, however, also potential disadvantages in these larger studies. Children's needs, deficits, problems and misdeeds are emphasised in counterproductive ways that can discourage general respect for children and young people and for their competencies and contributions. Longitudinal research, such as the 1958, 1970, 2000 birth cohorts conducted in the UK, relies on older questions and methods, which may not best suit children in the 2010s. The UK government supports much research about 'What Works?', meaning which services and interventions are most effective? These are tested by comparing two or more groups of people in trials. The aim is to have 'evidence based' planning and policy. This research tends to assume and promote adult control, values and cost-effective recommendations. If costs and cost-effectiveness are the priority, this can mean setting utility before principles and rights (see Boxes 1.7 and 1.8).

Relations between the social scientists, who produce evidence, and the politicians, who select, interpret and use the evidence to support their policies, can be strained. For example, urgent political requirements demand short-term evaluations with expedient, cost-effective and voter-friendly results. Yet on parenting programmes, for example, results may be too premature and 'weak' to provide the necessary evidence that politicians claim to offer. Attention to the majority can overlook the different needs and interests of minorities, for whom services may be working less well. Although the British Sure Start programme, for example, was designed to help disadvantaged young families, it appears to be least helpful to those in greatest need of support, the youngest single mothers (Rutter, 2008), though this is seldom admitted. These are only a few of the ways in which economics can complicate every stage of research, from first plans to final implementation. They are noted here for researchers who are affected by them to consider as part of their review of the ethics of their research.

Ethics and funding sources

Researchers sometimes have to decide whether or not to accept research funding from sources that may be unethical, such as companies whose products harm children.

Carbon costs

The UN (2009) reported that an estimated 211 million people were severely harmed by the effects of climate change during 2008. An editorial in the *British Medical Journal* points out that 'most of the health burden of climate change is borne by children in developing countries' from malnutrition, disease and flooding (Roberts and Godlee, 2007: 324–5; IPCC, 2007). The authors estimated that over 10,779 tonnes of carbon were emitted by 15,000 delegates travelling to one American Thoracic Society conference. This approximately equalled the annual carbon emissions or 'footprint' of around 550 Americans, 11,000 people in India and 110,000 people in Chad. Roberts and Godlee regard this as an ethical matter and conclude that 'doctors must lead by example' and find alternative ways to convene international conferences.

There are online research-related conferences and websites, with lecture and chatrooms, and videos of main lectures and panels discussions. The lecture texts, PowerPoint and oral presentations and the posters can be put online for several months, with space for emailed comments and debates. Virtual conferences can last much longer than real ones. They leave more detailed records to be downloaded, they are open to many more people than those who can afford the time and fares to travel, and can be accessed at any times which suit each 'delegate'.

The Sustainable Trials Study Group (2007) is linked to the worldwide Cochrane Collaboration, which conducts systematic reviews. Their aim is to discover the best evidence from all known relevant research in hundreds of topic areas. The Study Group conducted a carbon audit of a clinical trial held in 49 countries during 1999–2004. They estimated that in one year, 2003–2004, 126 tonnes of greenhouse gases were emitted by the research offices, staff travel and distribution of the trial drugs and materials. The report suggested ways to cut carbon emissions during medical research.

British universities are expected to 'take the lead' and to begin now, in line with European and national policies, towards cutting carbon emissions by at least 80 per cent by 2050 (www.hefce.ac.uk/susdevresources/carbon/).

The policy has five aims linked to ethics:

(1) to reduce carbon-related climate change and its effects;
(2) to conserve non-renewable resources for crucial uses, such as oil for plastics;
(3) to prevent the social disorder and conflict that will occur when carbon fuels become too scarce and expensive for most people to use, and societies still mainly depend on them for all aspects of daily life;
(4) to accelerate development of renewable energy resources;
(5) and through renewables and other measures to prepare systems that will support the predicted rise in population from around 6.7 billion now to 9 billion in 2050.

Pearce (2010) predicts that population growth is already levelling off, and will not reach nine billion. He argues that in any case population increase in the most deprived societies is not a threat to climate change or to human survival, when many people live not only at zero carbon levels but minus carbon levels, when their work is mainly, for example, picking rubbish, recycling or forestry. Instead, Pearce thinks, the main threat is from minority world small families who are wealthy high consumers (Gorringe, 1999; Shiva, 2000; Miller, 2002; Plumwood, 2002; Monbiot, 2006; Stephens, 2006; Lynas, 2007; Kempf, 2008; Bell, 2009; Giddens, 2009).

Carbon costs directly relate to the ethics of research with children because:

- those who are being and will be most severely affected by the effects of carbon-related climate change are younger and future generations;
- the present and potential effects on children are under-researched;
- and therefore through their selection of topics as well as their energy-consuming research processes researchers can influence public debates, policies and practices in positive or negative ways.

Ethics and contracts

The funding contract can have powerful effects on the ethics of each project. Management and budgeting involve the efficient and also ethical treatment of the whole research team with care and respect enabling them all to respect the participants, to develop their own ideas, analyse data in depth, and report the research widely.

If research teams are too hierarchical, it can be harder for junior researchers, who usually work most closely with the young participants, to report any problems they may have, and to get team leaders to attend to these problems. Most unfortunately, some junior researchers report that their concerns about their research project being unethical and exploiting children and young people, are dismissed by senior researchers who say, 'The research ethics committee approved the research and therefore there are no problems' (see Chapter 6).

Contracts with funders for research, consultancies and evaluations may need to allow for:

- reasonable costing and timing, including funds to allow for inclusive methods, such as the extra time and resources that may be needed for children who speak little or no English, and for children with learning difficulties (Braille, signing or IT communication, taxi and escort fares);
- regular discussion times among the research team;
- adequate secretarial, technical and library support, and project accommodation;
- a pilot or flexible initial period to learn from the research participants' responses and then possibly to improve the study design;
- time to collect and analyse the evidence;
- time to report back to the children and young people;
- time to write reports for all who have helped with the research, and for wide dissemination to increase the chance that useful findings might be implemented or might affect policies and attitudes;
- a freedom to publish clause (see below).

Research governance standards are promoting generally higher agreed standards in contracts, which may include funds for a sponsor or advisory group to oversee the progress of each research project. Contracts could include clauses on:

- the researchers' priorities and values;
- ethical questions raised by the research and the means of addressing these;
- an equal opportunities policy, and how cultural, religious, gender, age, disability or other differences among researchers and participants are respected;
- a disclaimer for funders in reports, saying that sponsorship does not necessarily mean support for the conclusions;
- researchers' intentions to report research problems and actual methods honestly;
- caution about how reliable and generalisable or transferable the data are likely to be;
- avoidance of fabrication and misrepresentation of data;
- final reports to be in sufficient detail to enable other researchers to understand and learn from the study;
- a freedom to publish and copyright clause.

Freedom to publish

Freedom to publish clauses prevent funders or researchers, research institutions or the agencies that have been researched, from refusing to allow the detailed findings to be published. They help to protect the integrity of the research. The National Children's Bureau Guidelines (1993; slightly less clearly in the newer 2003 version) state that in exceptional cases:

> Where we approach to undertake a study of a confidential or particularly sensitive area [plans for research reports] would need to be agreed between the Bureau and the funding agency at the outset. All reports will be shown to participating organisations and the funding agency in draft form and any comments will be carefully considered. [The Bureau] retains the responsibility for what is finally written [and] copyright, except where agreed otherwise. Evaluative research in particular, by its very nature, will often raise questions concerning certain existing policies or practices. This will always be presented constructively but participating agencies must be prepared for this possibility.

Researchers may produce important but disturbing findings that their own employers do not wish to publish, for fear of alienating patrons or funders. Contracts guard against this when they mention researchers' (and not only their agencies' or employers') rights to publish. However, another barrier to this freedom is having to satisfy editors, and in academic journals the peer reviewers, before publishing reports in the press. Many unexpected problems may arise during research. Foresight, well-thought-out contracts, and attention to ethical questions can all partly help to prevent or reduce these problems. This chapter concludes by considering payments for young people.

Paying young researchers and participants

Payments may be made for several reasons:

- to reimburse expenses, including escorts' fares;
- to compensate for time, inconvenience and possible discomfort;
- to show a token appreciation for participants' help;
- to pay for young people's help just as adults are paid;
- to recompense people who would have been earning by working or begging if they had not been helping with the research.

These payments can be ethical 'fair returns' for young participants' and young researchers' contributions to the research. Some guidelines advise that payments may be made to encourage participants to take part 'as an incentive'. However, they contravene the *Nuremberg* standards that no persuasion or pressure of any kind should be put on participants. Yet any payments, however fair, may still bribe or even coerce people into taking part. A payment that may be small to some people can be high for others, including disadvantaged people and many children. They may then feel pressured into accepting payment and feeling that they have to divulge more than they would choose to say, or say more strongly what they think researchers want to hear.

Should people be paid at the start and assured that, whatever they say or do, such as leave the study, the payment stands? Or should payment only be given 'as a surprise' afterwards, when there would be no risk of bribing people? Some funders do not allow payments to be made. However, on the importance of respecting and rewarding young people, see Box 7.5.

The advantages and disadvantages of paying young people are debated in a review of ethics guidelines (Wendler et al., 2002) that usefully separates the four types of payment – reimbursement, compensation, appreciation and incentive. The review concludes with 11 safeguards, given here for readers to debate. The safeguards aim to reduce the chance that parents' and children's decisions, about whether to join a study, will be distorted by promise of a payment.

(1) Develop guidelines for all four types of payment.
(2) Adopt an explicit policy on advertising payment to children.
(3) Require explicit justification for all incentives.
(4) Allow that children are paid less than adults in identical studies.
(5) Ensure payment to subjects who withdraw.
(6) Consider carefully any cases when there is concern that people are consenting because of payment and not because they wish to take part.
(7) Develop a general policy on describing payments in consent and assent forms.
(8) Make direct payments to the proper party.
(9) Avoid lump sum payments.

(10) Consider deferred payments.
(11) Consider non-cash payments.

Children in Scotland (2001: section 4) give another example of guidance on payment.

> Children in Scotland will refund all reasonable travel and subsistence expenses incurred by informants in the course of participating in the research, on production of receipts.
>
> Children in Scotland may also pay research contacts [participants] in addition to expenses as inducement to participate, as recompense for time, or as appreciation of the contribution. It may be made in the form of cash, vouchers, or in the form of a donation or gift to a group, school or other organisation. In survey research a prize draw may be used as an inducement to return the form.

Readers may wish to discuss the mention of 'inducement' and also the 'prize draw'. Although almost everyone supports lotteries, some people do not, and does this complicate the aims that the research be inclusive? One safeguard is when researchers alone do not have to make all the ethics decisions, but can share them with an ethics review committee, as considered in Chapter 6.

Payments in context

Research with children (and adults) in very poor or precarious situations, or where people mainly give or exchange practical help and things, rather than money, raises difficult questions about how to compensate people for their time. Payment can lead to misunderstandings and embarrassment between researchers and participants and others who help with the research. The question of payment needs to be understood in context. Sime (2008) discusses using gift vouchers as tokens of thanks in research with disadvantaged children in the UK. Vakaoti (2009) paid street children in Suva, Fiji, and gave them cinema vouchers.

Payment may be made in kind instead of in cash, such as giving school children pencils, pens and notebooks. One PhD student, Natalia Streuli, based in London and carrying out research in the Peruvian highlands, noticed how when she gave the children refreshments during the research activities, they carefully wrapped any leftovers to take home to their families. The next day, they came with plastic boxes so that could take any more leftovers, reflecting not only local norms that children contribute to the family economy, but also that reciprocity seemed to be very valuable to these families (Streuli, 2010).

Box 5.1   Young Lives

http://www.younglives.org.uk

Based in Oxford UK, Young Lives is doing government sponsored research on child poverty with 12,000 children over 15 years in Ethiopia, India, Peru and Vietnam. Each country research team deals with payment in ways that reflect cultural contexts about the value of people's time, their willingness to help with research 'for the common good', their poverty and not having to miss a day's wages to spend time talking to researchers. Norms of reciprocity and community, and/or obeying the government affect people's participation. However, paying respondents may lead to confusion.

In Ethiopia, children were encouraged to use the money to buy school materials. Families living in extreme poverty at first perceived Young Lives as an aid agency giving out practical help and money. Later, researchers were careful to explain that the research 'project' does not provide any aid to communities or individuals (Tafere et al., 2009).

In Peru, researchers gave small gifts as a 'thank you', as well as some supplies to local schools. In India, research teams also provided some resources to schools, as requested by local community leaders, to benefit all the local children and, up to 2009, they did not directly pay the participants. However, some participants thought it was unfair, that their time was not paid when it was given to benefit everyone in the community.

Cultures are not fixed and, by 2010, the question of remuneration to Young Lives research respondents became increasingly important as economies become more market oriented. For example, in Andhra Pradesh India, the National Rural Employment Guarantee Scheme, which pays workers at least Rs.60/- (the equivalent of 75 pence or about US$1) for a morning's work, has recently been implemented. Whereas in the past, the opportunity cost of spending time talking to a researcher may have been zero, or respondents could carry out domestic chores or work on the farm while talking with researchers, they are now becoming more aware of the financial value of their time, and are more likely to expect payment. Thus, Young Lives has decided to pay participants for their time in subsequent research rounds in India and might do so in the other countries. Otherwise, people might refuse to participate in future, especially in urban areas where it is already difficult to keep people involved.

Poverty might induce children and adults to feel under great pressure to consent, and to continue in research unwillingly, in order to receive payment. Care has to be exercised. Some people suggest that children should not be paid to help in research, because of this potential pressure, and because it puts them in a contractual relationship and diminishes their freedom to withdraw. Poor people also usually have low status, which can further reduce their power to refuse or to withdraw. (We will discuss consent in Chapter 8.)

Meanwhile, poverty and associated low status raise questions to consider. What kind of relationship do you want to have with the people who help with your research and supply information? Is it simply a contractual relationship? Do you hope to have a relationship of trust and shared interest in the information supplied? How might these relationships affect and shape the information supplied? Perhaps the possibility of mixed motives could be raised. Here we are talking about the pragmatics of collecting good quality data as well as ethics. It could be argued that relationships of trust can only be mutual, and sustained within some reciprocity (see Chapter 9) and some equality of power. This is hard to sustain when researchers can be so much more powerful than participants, although that is why respect and consent are so vital (Chapter 8).

Researchers may have mixed motives when their 'principled' refusal to pay participants keeps down research budgets, reduces administration, and avoids potential disputes and bargaining about pay rates. An example from Zimbabwe questions whether people are more willing to be honest if they are paid, or if they feel that they should produce or invent extra responses to deserve the fee. Groceries were presented at the end of each interview, when one man became embarrassed. He said he had thought this was some kind of government survey, not the long-term study with which he was well acquainted. He told the interviewer to throw away his notes and start the interview again – this time he would tell the truth! (Michael Bourdillion, pers. comm., March 2010). The example points to the vital need to establish the right kinds of relationships, those which produce reliable information.

Box 5.2   Fieldwork in Ethiopia

Tatek Abebe (2009: 461) describes how:

Conducting fieldwork among economically disadvantaged children as a privileged, educated, car-driving man raised complex personal questions relating to material inequalities. As most of the participants were from low-income groups and many of them, including child beggars, move in different places to earn their daily income, I believed ... that giving them some money was adequate reward for their time and labour, and hopefully a way of encouraging their participation. In schools, I gave or paid for children's stationery materials. On streets, I gave money to children, and paid for the meals we frequently shared.

However, my relationships with many of the children were deep and mutual. The children bought me gifts on different occasions, invited me to their houses,

(Continued)

(Continued)

shared their food with me ... Looking at the contexts of deep-seated poverty and harsh material deprivation, I became compelled not to detach myself from their circumstances. Although I never made any promises for the future, (temporary) reciprocal relationships have nurtured the research space in many fruitful ways ... reciprocity ... reflects how ethical spatiality is the product of interrelationships ... and that dominant ethical principles are actually lived in, reproduced and experienced by research participants through interactions.

Summary of questions

- Should the research funds be raised only from agencies that avoid activities that can harm children?
- Does the funding allow for time and resources to enable researchers to liaise adequately with the children, and to collect, collate and analyse the data efficiently and accurately?
- Are the children's and parent's or carers' expenses repaid?
- Should children be paid or given some reward after helping with research?

Six

Reviewing aims and methods: ethics guidance and committees

This chapter concerns applying to research ethics committees (RECs) and making the final revisions to research plans, perhaps after pilots, or in the light of comments from colleagues and other reviewers. For decades, medical research has been informed by REC or IRB reviews and detailed ethics guidelines, and social research is following this example. However, are review committees and guidance useful, and could they be more so? As we noted earlier, one aim of this book is to promote discussion among social researchers about the value of collective reviews and guidance (Alderson and Morrow, 2006; Munro, 2008).

Review and revision of research aims and methods

It is now more generally accepted that children and young people have a great deal of knowledge, which can be very useful at all stages of a research project and not simply during the data collecting phases (Hill, 2004). Research that is seriously planned with 'insider' experienced children, young people and adults is perhaps more likely to involve relevant questions and ethical methods.

Consultation with users and other reviewers ranges from informal contacts, to committee reviews, to conducting formal pilots. Most researchers now have to apply to an REC or IRB for approval before they can begin to contact participants. We suggest that there should always be a stage in any research when a group reviews the planned research to see if it is ethical and to ask:

- Are the basic assumptions about children underlying the research positive?
- Is there scope for taking real account of children's and adults' comments, and their complaints if these arise?
- Who are the researchers accountable to when they justify their work?

Children can advise on a wide range of methods, as recommended in Box 6.1.

Box 6.1   Involving children in designing research to promote good science and ethics

A systematic overview of research reports about barriers to and facilitators for children's physical activity started with 8231 titles and abstracts. The reviewers found that only 69 of the reported programmes had been properly evaluated. And only five evaluations actually showed whether the programmes worked or not – a great waste of resources and opportunities. The review team also concluded that children's own views are rarely heard so that basic data are missing (Brunton et al., 2003: 104). The team recommended that the views of children, aged 4–10 years, 'should be the starting point for any future development of efforts to promote physical activity ... Where possible children should be asked directly for their views on what could or should be done to promote their ... activity ... Children, parents and other stakeholders should be involved in planning the evaluation of interventions to physical activity ... in determining relevant and appropriate data collection methods, tools and topics, and in determining outcomes to be measured.' The team counted parents' replies on behalf of their children as parents' views (and not necessarily as children's), and said that studies 'need to engage children in a way that honours them as research participants [and] in a dialogue that is meaningful to them' (Brunton et al., 2003: 102–4).

Does social research need research ethics committees?

Do RECs/IRBs help to raise standards of social research? There are arguments for and against the review committees, mainly based on the debates about medical RECs but which could be considered in relation to social RECs for reviewing research, consultations and evaluations.

How are research ethics committees useful?

RECs can help to prevent poor research, safeguard research participants and be a protective barrier between potential participants and researchers. They help to raise awareness and serious concern about research ethics. One effect is that many researchers now consider ethics to be a basic part of research planning and processes, not just an afterthought. By involving 'lay' people, service users and people from different disciplines (such as law, philosophy, religion, social science) among their members, medical RECs encourage researchers to be challenged, to take account of differing views and values, and to be accountable.

Some RECs, especially those in healthcare, show that a single committee can cover studies involving a range of disciplines/professions, methods, theories and topics; it not necessary, and may not be beneficial, to have RECs, which review too narrow a range of disciplines and methods and lack inter-disciplinary questions and challenges. RECs, especially the 'lay' members who should represent participants, help to raise standards of clear information for research participants by vetting research information sheets and local RECs can check that the research suits their area, stop certain groups being over-researched, and see if leaflets in other languages and link-workers should be in the research plans.

Although this is now less common and reviews are more streamlined, if there is review by several RECs (for multi-centre projects), this can be a safeguard. Errors and harms overlooked by some RECs may be noticed by others.

Some disagreement among REC members about questions of ethics and values is inevitable, and can increase ethical awareness through practical debate about actual protocols.

How are research ethics committees not useful?

RECs may waste research time and money, especially when multi-centre research has to be submitted to many committees. They can delay research for months and seriously disrupt contracts and staffing, although fortunately this is now less common and RECs usually have to meet firm deadlines. There are seldom formally allocated funds for the sometimes high costs of applying to RECs.

RECs are under-funded and rely on many hours of unpaid work. They can be inefficient. Some lack the experts needed for proper review. Medical RECs charge high rates for drug companies applications, which subsidise other applications. Yet there is concern that the generous pharmacy funding, to run RECs and train members, can compromise RECs' independence.

RECs cannot completely guarantee that ethical research is supported and poor research prevented, with the added danger that their reported approval stops proper criticism.

Some RECs nit-pick over small points, and disagree with other committees' decisions about protocols, which suggests that REC review is inefficient and unscientific.

Social researchers complain that some RECs do not understand all main social research approaches and methods and do not have enough regular or co-opted expert members. RECs can be dominated by a few members who are determined to accept or reject certain protocols.

There is a serious danger that researchers may pass on ethical responsibility to RECs, and conduct research which they privately believe is useless or harmful, arguing in public that 'it must be all right, it has been approved' (Sylvester and Green, 2003).

Institutional problems with research ethics committees

REC members may also feel unhappily that they are made to appear to support research, and are forced to grant approval, by arguments about time and financial pressures from the researchers, from other REC members, or from their institution.

RECs at times end up contradicting their original purpose, by endorsing and supporting unethical research. Consent (Chapter 8) is like a fine-grained sieve, when each potential participant should be free to decide if they wish to take part in the research. The earlier broader-grained sieving is also vital, when RECs either pass or hold back protocols. They may pass some they are not entirely happy with, assuming that later people can freely choose and refuse. However, the REC's approval can itself undermine and mislead potential participants' later freedom to refuse. When we invited comments while writing this book, some junior researchers, in closest contact with participants, said it was hard for them to get the senior researchers and managers to take ethical criticisms and problems seriously and not simply to reply that the REC had approved the research.

We are very concerned about the serious problem of RECs approving too many studies. We can only suggest that the REC chair or administrator should be ready to deal with reported concerns about approved research. However, the growing business-style pressures to process funded research can severely inhibit the freedoms of RECs members, researchers and participants. Conversely, some would argue that RECs overly restrict research with children and young people, when they do not allow research with young people to be done without parental consent (see Chapter 8 and Skelton, 2008).

Recent experiences with research ethics committees

When we invited contributions to the book, we received some criticisms about RECs in relation to early years research. These criticisms are listed here with our responses in italics.

(1)   The role of the REC is to give informed advice on the ethical implications of the study.
Reply.   *RECs also have to assess protocols against agreed standards and grant approval or ask for improvements.*

(2)   The REC does not know the setting, or the kind of participants, or the exact legislation and ethics guidance on good practice within specific disciplines.
Reply.   *If the REC members seem to be ignorant or unrealistic, you could ask them to invite an expert in your speciality to join the committee, or at least to advise them.*

(3)   The REC standards for consent contradicted the usual practice in the settings, and one setting carried out their customary practice instead, deeming this to be more supportive of parents'/carers' understanding of the research and therefore less cause for concern.

Reply.   There seem to be some contradictions here. (a) Does the 'usual practice' refer to requests for consent to research or, very different, consent to care and other provision for the children? (b) If consent to research is 'usual' implying 'often', it seems odd that the centre is not more aware of consent standards. (c) If there is likely to be 'cause for concern' and if parents, and presumably children too, need 'support', then there is even more reason to inform parents and children and to ask for their consent (see Chapters 2, 7 and 8).

(4)   The two different standards of consent 'set up a conflict of beneficence'.

Reply.   Care-giving, teaching and providing other services involve beneficence but research does not; the children help the researchers (see Chapters 2 and 8, double standards).

(5)   The REC framework may not allow for consideration of the importance of the special relationship between practitioners and parents/carers that has long been recognised as critical to the effective provision of care and education, an ethic of care is required to foster a mutually respectful relationship as explicitly stated in the Early Years Foundation Stage document (DCSF, 2008).

Reply.   Relationships of mutual respect and trust are indeed vital, and are fostered during the honest exchange of information, questioning and discussion. Trust is undermined if parents are not informed, especially if they discover a cover up. This is even more crucial in research than when providing care and, again, the differences between research and practice need to be understood (see Chapters 2, 7 and 8). It is implied that the researcher is also a practitioner (see Introduction on the complications of researchers being 'insiders').

(6)   If an ethical framework that has evolved from a bio-medical model is imposed, that may not allow for important practitioner–parent relationships to influence the research design.

Reply.   RECs usually support participants being involved in designing research, including health care research, and especially in writing the information leaflets when other plans can also be discussed. The biomedical ethics model of honestly informing people and respecting their consent leads the way in helping to ensure people's informed willing cooperation and indeed commitment to the research.

(7)   The avoidance of preventable harm resulting from a medical procedure, such as the use of human tissue, does not necessarily inform the design of a social research project where one of the major considerations is to support positive and honest relationships within the researched community.

Reply.   Whereas invasive biomedical research risks damage to bodies, intrusive social research risks disrupting people's lives, relationships and opportunities (for example, if they are involved in a teaching study that turns out to hold children back and waste their time). There are risks not only during social research data collection, but also in how research is analysed, reported and publicised if, for example, people think they have been misreported or disrespected. This can leave people feeling seriously harmed and wronged. Physical and mental harm overlap when the worst effects of bodily injury from research may be emotional or social, and serious harm from social research may be felt physically as painful distress. There is not one objective standard of risk. People's views about what is risky vary and cannot easily be predicted. These are all reasons for researchers to be careful to think about potential risks and explain them before asking for consent (Chapters 2, 3 and 7). The repeated emphasis on protecting present relationships raises questions about how strong and honest these are.

(8)   The dangers of a paternalistic 'doing to' approach are not to be under-estimated.

Reply.   *Yes and that is why respectful informed consent is so vital (Chapters 7 and 8).*

(9)   Practitioners gave fully informed consent but not the children. Staff were reassured that the children, not the staff, would be observed and recorded.

Reply.   *RECs usually aim to respect everyone involved and it is especially vital to inform and respect the people who are most involved, in this case the children (Chapter 8).*

(10)   Observation is an integral part of early years practitioners' work with children.

Reply.   *Yes, it is part of the routine work, but observations for research serve different purposes (see Introduction and Chapters 1, 2 and 3). (Furthermore see Chapter 3 on why the opt out approach exerts more pressure.)*

(11)   In one setting, the REC insisted that a non-consent form was posted to parents/carers instead of, as usual with all other notes from the centre to parents, being given to the children to take home. The researcher wanted the REC to understand that posted letters could alarm parents, leave ones with few reading skills feeling confused and anxious, demand administrative time from staff who had to address the stamped addressed envelopes as the researcher could not see the lists of addresses. In contrast, giving out the forms when the children went home saved time and costs, was more low key, informal and friendly, and staff could explain to parents who did not read much.

Reply.   *These are all important useful points and show the value of RECs working flexibly with researchers on detailed sensitive ways to carry out general standards. However, the 'non-consent' form is not a recognised approach and risks intimidating people. Proper forms recognise people's rights to give or to withhold their consent.*

(12)   Can observations be truly non-participant if children know they are being observed? Observers can stand apart and avoid eye contact (Cohen et al., 2000). But the very presence of the observer will impact on the actions of the children and there is a need for this to be acknowledged in the research design and its limitations.

Reply.   *Yes, for decades researchers have tended to agree that it is not possible for observers to behave like an invisible fly on the wall. To avoid eye contact and ignore children who speak to you is neither good research method nor good ethics. It is easier for researchers to merge into the group, until after a while adults and children take little notice of them and carry on much as usual, if researchers introduce themselves, explain what they are doing, and reply to questions and other conversation. Interactions between researchers and participants are part of the data and not necessarily 'a limitation'. Careful analysis examines their possible effects and how these might increase understanding, rather than pretending the effects do not exist.*

(13)   An insistence by the REC that full, unconditional ethical approval is met before the research is begun negates the concept of ethics being an integral part of the whole research process.

Reply.   *We hope that our ten chapters on the ten stages of research show the value of detailed ethics planning, formal REC ethics approval, and then careful references to the agreed insights and standards through the rest of the research project. If major changes are necessary later, RECs review these. If reapplication is too complicated and slow, we hope that researchers can negotiate better terms with the REC or with the Director or Dean or Manager responsible for the REC.*

(14)   The REC insisted that no approach could be made to potential participant institutions before ethics approval was obtained. The researcher then imposes their predetermined design, rather than having the freedom to co-construct the design with practitioners, children or parents/carers.

Reply.   *If researchers fortunately have the time and funding to be able to work on co-constructing research designs with participants, or to do a formal pilot, they can put in a short application to the REC for this initial stage, with an information leaflet that sets out the aims, plans, timing, uncertainties, questions to be covered, position of the helping participants, and whether or not their institution might be in the full study.*

One way to test research ethics standards is to consider whether you would be happy to consent for yourself, or for a child. Would you mind, if you were the parent of a four-year-old, if strangers you knew nothing about were researching with him or her without informing you? Would you want to set any limits on what they might do? How would you respond if your child asked you questions about the research?

Researchers who sent us comments on applying to RECs mentioned the advantages of having to clarify: the researchers' roles; their aims and methods; their information to the different groups involved with the research; their respect for consent and refusal. The main disadvantages are with the time, effort and delay involved with applications, and with REC comments and queries that researchers believe to be ignorant or trivial.

Ethics reviews attempt to balance rigorous science with humane respect and compassion, and to balance the interests of present research participants with those of people who might benefit in future. This is partly why RECs sometimes disagree, depending on their memberships. There is not necessarily a correct way to balance conflicting values. The process of working towards reasonable, or least harmful, solutions can help to develop higher ethical standards, and to reach some consensus.

The former double standard, when healthcare research had to pass through REC vetting, and social research did not, is now largely resolved in universities. Some larger children's charities now have ethics committees. Yet it still applies in much commercial and small agency research and in some government departments, when social research does not go through any ethics review. To be effective, and to be widely established and respected, many social RECs need to address the following questions, some of which are still unresolved among healthcare RECs.

- How can the purpose and remit of the RECs be agreed or at least respected by all the researchers who apply to them?

- How can reasonable ethical standards and assessment criteria for all the varied disciplines and research methods be agreed?
- How can conflict and rivalry between members be prevented from skewing REC decisions?

Other ways to promote thinking about ethics before and during research studies include having an advisory group, and having regular research team meetings with a slot for ethics or for clarifying and working to resolve general critical concerns. In hierarchical and large research teams, it is vital that senior staff take junior researchers' concerns seriously. There might be an anonymous suggestions box. Teams might invite an outsider to chair some team meetings to help to ensure that there is fair and detailed discussion about difficulties.

International standards

There is growing concern about double standards when minority world RECs/IRBs demand high standards but research in other countries may have little or no ethical scrutiny or accountability (see the Pfizer example in Chapter 8). Nationally and internationally, networks between review committees help to raise and maintain standards, including in research-active countries national associations of the sociologists, psychologists, anthropologists, social policy researchers, statisticians and economists. Their websites and latest updated guidance are probably best found on search engines. For example, in the UK: AREC (Association of Research Ethics Committees) publishes a journal and convenes regular meetings (www.arec.org.uk); the Department of Health (2004), and the main research councils (www.esrc.ac.uk) publish guidelines. The Wellcome Trust funds research in the UK and abroad, and issues guidance on the ethics of genetic research, for example, which raises vital social and moral questions. Most of the work on reconciling international standards concerns biomedical research, but it is highly relevant in much of its research content and processes to social research too.

Work to align standards of research conducted between minority and majority world countries include the Wellcome Trust's discussion paper based on a workshop held in South Africa 2004. The Trust supports the work of the Africa Centre for Health and Populations Studies (www.africacentre.ac.za), and for the study of the ethics of anthropologies of African biosciences (Molyneux and Geissler, 2008; http://aab.lshtm.ac.uk/?q=node/47).

Also based in London and part-funded by the Wellcome Trust, The Nuffield Council on Bioethics (2002, 2005), has published two reports on research in majority world countries which advise on research ethics. The Council recommends that international protocols are reviewed in every country involved, not just one country to stand in for the rest. These are some of the standards set for researchers in the 2002 report.

- Understand local traditions, when seeking consent. Often consultation with the community is as important as gaining the consent of individual trial participants.
- Design information sheets and consent forms to assist potential participants to make informed choices. We recommend that the information provided should be accurate, concise, clear, simple, specific to the proposed research and appropriate for the social and cultural context (2002: 6.40).
- If it is not possible to obtain written consent, record genuine oral consent on audio tape, provided the researcher and an independent witness sign an extra form that has been approved by the research ethics committee (2002: 6.39).
- Strengthen local capacity to review research ethics, in order to ensure that reviewers take account of local knowledge and interests, and tailor research to fit the local population.
- Adapt strict adherence with ethics guidelines to meet local needs when necessary.
- Plan standards of care and also any care after the trial is over, and agree contentious matters at an early stage between all the agencies concerned: researchers, health authorities, funders and governments.
- Before the trial begins, endeavour to secure agreement from the funding body that participants will have post-trial access to effective interventions. The lack of such arrangements should have to be justified to a research ethics committee (2002: 9.31).

Other examples from numerous networks include the UK Medical Research Council joint African-European programme to promote ethics and identify present capacity, and the Indian Medical Research Council's work with the USA (www.icmr.nic.in/guide.htm) and the US Office for Human Research Protections (www.hhs.gov/ohrp/international/).

A national social research ethics forum?

In recent years, there has been progress on designing and updating ethics codes by funders and by professional associations (see References). However, there is currently no respected national multidisciplinary social research forum covering the range of agencies, disciplines and methods to debate ethical problems, and potentially to aid progress towards resolving problems and promoting higher standards. Medical RECs have a central body (www.arec.org.uk). As already mentioned, people who criticise current standards in research ethics may be isolated and have no collective political voice. Chapter 11 reviews some questions that social researchers cannot resolve on their own. This is a fast changing field, and guidance is frequently produced and revised. However, a respected social science research central forum could:

- continue to summarise and synthesise new changes in national and international policies;
- bring researchers up to date on major changes;

- explain and justify the practical meaning of these changes and how they affect everyday social research and consultations;
- help to agree reasonable standards and answers to ethical dilemmas;
- and so help to protect participants, researchers and the good name of social research;
- coordinate and validate training programmes for social researchers and REC members;
- liaise with medical and other RECs to support positive coordination and to avoid wasteful duplication of review – which has been much reduced quite recently.

Summary of questions

- Have children or their carers helped to plan or comment on the research?
- Has a committee, a small group or an individual reviewed the protocol specifically for its ethical aspects and approach to children?
- Is the design in any way unhelpful or unkind to children? For example, are they asked to do activities or talk about matters that embarrass or humiliate or pain or confuse them? Are they deceived? Are the questions and the research reports mainly about problems and failings in their lives?
- Is there scope for taking account of comments and improving the research design?
- Are the researchers accountable to anyone, to justify their work?
- What are the agreed methods of dealing with complaints?

PART 2

The data collecting stage

Seven

Information

Although similar ethical questions overlap through all the stages of research, evaluation or consultation, certain questions are most pressing during periods of direct contact with participants. These are highlighted in Part 2, Chapters 7 and 8. Chapter 7 summarises the main details that people who are asked to take part in research need to know in order to be able to give informed consent. It is vital to inform people of all ages clearly.

Spoken and written information

Whether children and adults can or cannot read or choose to read the information leaflets, it is still important that:

- researchers or mediators/interpreters spend time orally explaining the research, while taking care to avoid any pressure (see Chapter 8); and
- research teams use an agreed short information leaflet and go through explaining and checking that people understand.

When all the researchers in a team use the same leaflet, or the same local translation, this can help to ensure that accurate, carefully worked out and standardised information is given. This respects children's rights to information (UNCRC Articles 13 and 17) and freedom of thought and conscience (Article 14) by enabling them to form their own views (Article 12) before deciding about consent (see Chapter 8). There is also respect for parents and other carers (Article 20) in their rights and duties 'to provide direction to the child ... in a manner consistent with the evolving capacities of the child' (Articles 14 and 5) and to further 'the best interests of the child' (Articles 3 and 18). Although there is concern that parents prevent children who wish to do so from taking part in research, there are also examples of dangerous research, which it is better to refuse to take part in, in order to protect the child's health (Article 24) and occasionally even the child's survival (Article 6; Stephens 2006; www.business-humanrights.org 2009), children's standard of living (Article 27) and development (Article 29), also to prevent discrimination (Article 2), abuse and exploitation (Articles 19, 32, 36 and 37; and see Cooter, 1992; Sharav, 2003; Coppock, 2005; Ross, 2006; Baughman, 2007;

Slesser and Qureshi, 2009). Research may interfere unlawfully with privacy, or may attack the child's honour and reputation (Article 17). RECs are quasi-legal committees, whose decisions are taken as legal evidence if the researchers are taken to court, so that RECs have the duty to see that the research is 'lawful' in its remit and methods.

Research information leaflets

The details about research projects can be set out in simple leaflets. These are also a useful basis for talking about the research and answering further questions with each participant. One way to avoid either under- or over-informing (boring, confusing) people is to put a core of basic information in the leaflet, with suggestions for further topics to discuss. This can combine what the reasonable researcher would tell, what a prudent person would ask, and what each individual wants to know. Ethics committees usually require to see such leaflets, as the only means of checking that potential participants receive at least basic information. When writing leaflets, researchers could talk with the people they are planned for. What questions do they want to be raised? What terms do they use?

The leaflets can be given to everyone affected by the research as a short handy guide: to children and young people, parents and carers, other adults such as staff in the school or wherever the research takes place, and to general enquirers. If the same leaflet is clear enough for young children or people with learning difficulties, it can be used for everyone. Such leaflets could also be used by many adults working with or caring for children when they are doing research, evaluations or routine assessments or case studies, or by journalists making a documentary, or psychologists doing statements with children who have special needs. Simple leaflets can help to overcome ignorance, resistance and even fear, and can encourage more efficient and respectful working relationships between adults and children and young people.

The leaflets can explain who you are, what you are doing, why and how. This helps children to be prepared and to feel more in control over what is happening. Yet it is important not to assume that people read or remember the leaflets. Researchers need to talk through the leaflets with children and leave plenty of pauses for questions. Leaflets are an extra resource, and cannot replace discussion. Leaflets often start with what the researcher wants to tell. Instead, it is better to put yourself in the children's position and begin by explaining what they might most want to know.

Leaflets and discussions with children who might join the research can include the details in Box 7.1. Some of these points have been covered in earlier chapters, but they are listed here as items to explain to participants. (See also Box 2.1 on risk–benefit, Chapter 3 on privacy and Chapter 8 on consent and refusal rights.)

Box 7.1 Title, topics and purpose

Title

Apart from a formal title, does the study have a simple user-friendly, working title? 'A survey commissioned by the local authority social services department of out-of-school provision for children aged 4 to 11 years' hardly sounds inviting. Children stress that they like the clubs to be as different from school as possible, and this can include renaming their centre from 'out-of-school' to 'The Palace'. 'The Palace Project' is likely to attract more interest, and to help young people to feel more involved.

Topics

What are the main topics areas?
What are the main questions?
Many young people aged under 16 become homeless.
We hope to learn from them about what kinds of help they need.

Or:

Each year, many young people are excluded from their school. Why does this happen? We are asking young people, parents and teachers for their views.

Or:

Some people in this school have problems with maths. We want to try out a new maths course. Will you help us?

Purpose/aims

What is the point of asking the questions?
What do the researchers hope to achieve? To add to knowledge, to inform policy?
How is the research worthwhile?
How are the findings likely to benefit children? (For example?)
What new questions does this research ask which no other research has yet answered?

Box 7.2   What will happen to people during the research?

- How long will the research take?
- For how much time will each person will be involved?
- How many sessions there will be and where?
- How often and how long will or might the sessions be?

(Continued)

(Continued)

Methods

- What methods will be used? (For example, a tape-recorded interview, a survey, a maths programme, counselling sessions, observations, focus groups, questionnaires, a randomised trial.)
- What kinds of questions might be asked? Open or closed or both? To question experiences or views? To enquire after public or personal matters?
- Do the research methods need to be explained and justified? For example:
  - Are relevant research terms, such as 'randomised' or 'control group' explained?
  - Why is the chosen method the preferred one?

Box 7.3   Use of data

- How certain is it that each person's data will be used?
- In qualitative reports, for example, might some people be reported only very briefly or not at all?
- Will people be sent a transcript of their interview if they wish, for them to check and keep?
- Will their photographs or drawings be returned to them?
- When reports are being written, will people be asked to comment, especially if they might be identified or might disagree with the researchers' conclusions?

Box 7.4   Further information

Naming contacts
  The leaflet should include the names of:

- the researcher with telephone number/email;
- the research base with full address;
- the sponsors;
- the REC and the approved project number, if relevant.

RECs require leaflets:

- to state that research cannot offer direct benefits;
- to explain any risks or harms;
- to give details about researchers' indemnity – if there is serious harm who will pay any costs and compensation, this relates to medical rather than social research.

Leaflet layout

Clearly written and laid out information can help everyone concerned:

- to discuss the research more fully and clearly;
- to decide what questions to ask the researchers;
- to understand and remember researchers' spoken information;
- to know about the hoped for benefits of the research and any risks or costs.

Leaflets can help to increase informed public support for efficient research. They help funders and others who assess research, such as ethics committee members:

- to find out quickly and clearly the essential points about the research;
- to assess the value of the research, and the researchers' attitudes towards the participants.

The tone and style of the leaflet often are a good indication of this. Does it seem reader friendly?

The leaflet needs to be written in terms that children can read, or can understand when someone reads it to them. For some studies, a coloured sheet of A4 is folded to make four A5 pages. Narrow columns are much easier to read, as newsprint shows. A project logo might be added, and perhaps drawings, flow charts, spider diagrams, speech bubbles or other useful and cheerful diagrams, and a small photograph of the researchers. Large dark print on white or pale matt – not glossy – paper helps people with poor eyesight, as well as slow readers. Subheadings or a question and answer format also help them, with the messages broken up into short sections. A sheet with fuller details could be tucked inside the leaflet for complicated research studies.

Clear leaflets show that researchers want to think and write in terms young people prefer, and they allow for people who read little English. Plain language risks being crude, simplistic, patronising and irritating, but it can be worse to use confusing and intimidating language. Clear leaflets use:

- short lines, words, sentences and paragraphs;
- one main idea per sentence;
- requests rather than commands;
- the active voice (we will meet you …) rather than the passive voice (appointments will be booked);
- a personal approach (we, you, your sister) rather than the impersonal (they, those, he or she);
- specific details rather than vagueness.

The leaflets avoid repetition, negative remarks (do not …), alienating labels, jargon and acronyms unless they are explained. Some researchers use Maketon or other sign language to write leaflets for people with learning difficulties. Braille and audio-recorded information can be used for blind people, large print for those with partial sight.

Examples of research information leaflets

There follows on pages 91–94 an example of a leaflet designed for young children as they can be the hardest group to inform. The researchers interviewed children aged from 3 to 12 years, with their parents when they preferred a joint session. They aimed for a clear leaflet for children to read themselves, and for parents/carers to read with younger ones, explaining to them as much as they thought the child needed and wanted to know.

Leaflets in other languages

Translations need to be checked by two or three readers to see that they are clear and accurate, and for their tone and style. Ask one person to translate the text, and another to translate it back. Leaflets in other languages should be used with a link worker or interpreter, not used alone. Participants can then share their views with the researchers. Interpreters may block, rather than aid, discussion, unless they are well chosen; age, gender, empathy, respect for clients, skill in listening and some knowledge of the research can be vital. Research with people who speak little or no English should include funds for these services. There may be a local multi-cultural education advisory service that can help. However, there may still be problems about which dialect to use and local community groups may be able to help. One large study involved interpreters for 27 languages. In the follow up study, the researchers trained the interpreters to conduct the interviews themselves and to be full members of the research team (Oakley et al., 2003). Diagrams, flowcharts and other visual explanations are especially useful for overcoming language barriers.

Information in semi-literate societies

We mentioned at the beginning of this chapter the importance of research teams sharing the same basic leaflet or locally translated version. When few if any of the participants will read the leaflets, and researchers depend even more on spoken information, they benefit from training and practising before they start inviting people to join the research. Some teams have handbooks for all their researchers, which include ethics standards to observe.

An information leaflet for children and parents posted to them
at home by hospital staff

Living with diabetes

A research project

August – December 2003

This leaflet is for children

and their parents

Please will you help us with our research?

This leaflet gives some details about the project.
We have set out the questions you might want to ask,
with our answers, so you can talk about them together
before you decide if you would like to take part.

Please contact us, Katy or Priscilla,
if you want more details and/or
if you would like to join the project.
Katy Sutcliffe (phone and email)
Priscilla Alderson (phone and email)
(address)

Why is the research being done?

As you know, the way you care for yourself is vital to help you to keep healthy. But, so far, researchers have not asked children much about how they share in their own diabetes care.

We plan to listen to boys and girls, parents/carers, and health staff, and write reports about their views.

The aim is to help families and health care staff know more about the kinds of daily diabetes care that children and parents find work well.

What questions will the project ask?

* How do girls and boys with diabetes share in their daily health care, such as deciding what to eat and when?

* When are they old enough to do blood tests?

* Do you have any problems with diabetes? And, if so, how do you and your parents try to solve these?

* Do you remember when you first knew you had diabetes? Have there been any changes in your care since then? Would you like to make other changes?

* What do you find works well?

* How would you advise someone who has diabetes?

Who will be in the project?

Ten boys and girls at X ---- Hospital
and ten boys and girls at Y ---- Hospital, and their parents.
The age groups are 3–6 and 10–12 years.
Dr B-------- has chosen the children at your hospital to be asked to take part. He has not told us your names.

Do I have to take part?

You decide if you want to take part or not.

Even if you say 'yes', you can drop out at any time.

And you can tell us if you want to stop, or have a break.

If you don't want to answer some questions, just say 'pass'. You do not have to tell us anything unless you want to. And you don't have to give us a reason if you say 'no' or 'stop'. Whether you help us or not, you will still go on having just the same care at your hospital.

What will happen to me if I take part?

If you agree, one of us will meet you at your home, or at the clinic, to talk to you, and your mother or father. We would like to tape-record you. You might play some games and talk with us for between 15 to 60 minutes. We will not look for right or wrong answers, it is your own views that matter. Later, we'll ask you to test a question booklet we will be writing for other children.

Could there be any problems for me if I take part?

We hope you will enjoy talking to us. A few people get upset when talking about their lives, and if they want to stop, we stop. We can put them in touch with someone to help them, if they wish. If you have any complaints about the project, please tell us, or Dr B-----.

Will doing the research help me?

We hope you will like helping us. But our main aim is to write reports that will help very many families in the future. Maybe you too will find the reports useful.

Who will know if I am in the research, or what I have talked about?

Dr B------ will know if you are in the project, but we will not tell him or anyone else what you tell us.

The only time we might have to break this promise is if we think you or someone else might be at risk of being hurt. If so, we will talk to you first about the best thing to do.

We will keep our tapes and notes about you in a safe lockable place, and delete named details about you after the project.

When we write reports about your views, we will change your name, so no one will know you said that.

Will I know about the research results?

We will send you a short report in Spring 2004, and longer reports too, if you want to see them.

The project is funded by a Social Science Research Unit grant.

It was approved by X------- Hospital Research Ethics Committee, project no. 405, and by Dr B ------.

The researchers, Priscilla and Katy, carry out research and write reports and books about children's and parents' views on health care and education.

If you take part, please keep this leaflet with the copy of your consent form.

June 2003, leaflet version 1.

Thank you for reading this leaflet.

The Young Lives (2006: 12) fieldworker instruction handbook advises researchers to talk with children and 'explain in ways that they can understand why you are there, why you are interviewing them and what the information is to be used for'. The qualitative researchers are expected to be clear about the limited capacity of the research to bring about change in the participants' lives. Using local translations, they explain to children:

> Young Lives is a study of children growing up in four countries, India, Peru, Vietnam and Ethiopia, taking place over 15 years. We are trying to find out about children's everyday lives: the things you do, and the important people in your life, and how these things affect how you feel. Bits of what you say/write/draw will be used in reports that we write that we hope will be helpful to local and national governments when making plans or planning services for children in the future. Our research may not change things in the short term, because that depends on local and national governments. (Young Lives, n.d.: 1)

Relevant research?

In many parts of the world, however, people do not necessarily understand what research is, especially in three particular ways. First, the heavy practical demands of subsistence living and family care and survival can make it hard for them to imagine how and why other people have the time and money to be able to concentrate on ideas and talk, seemingly as ends in themselves. Second, people who have a basic education have little understanding of the nature and purpose of research knowledge and theories, data collection and analysis. Third, their experience of NGOs leads adults and children in very poor areas to expect that visiting adults will 'save' the children somehow. Abebe notes that, despite the fact that he explained that he was a researcher, 'if a child succeeds in becoming affiliated to an organisation, it becomes an important source of income for the household' (2009: 456).

Eric Orieno Nyambedha (2008), in his long-term study on the effects of the AIDS pandemic on orphans in western Kenya, also found that adults asked him:

> What are you going to do to the orphans after you have studied them? ... Many wanted to know whether my proposed research would 'take' the orphans ... (kawo nyithind kiye) a phrase used to refer to the activities of many NGOs in the neighbouring communities, involving sponsoring orphans to attend school by paying school fees and buying school uniforms ... because of the living conditions of people affected by AIDS, many people in the study area did not believe that somebody working closely with a European organisa-tion from the West could just come all the way from Nairobi to ask the orphans ... [and their widowed mothers] questions about their life without providing assistance. (Nyambedha, 2008: 773–4; see also Morrow, 2009)

The term orphans can mean that one parent has died and not necessarily both parents. In some countries there is great emphasis on the specific child–parent relationship and on parents' legal rights and proxy consent. In other countries there may be several carers with less emphasis on the individual parent, which will alter how researchers approach obtaining adults' consent for research with children.

Two-way information exchanged throughout the research study

Ethics guidance tends to see information giving as one-way: researchers inform potential participants. The process is more useful if it is two-way, when researchers listen to participants, sort out misunderstandings and discuss with them about how the research could be improved. Data collecting mainly involves children and young people informing the researchers. Towards the end of the study, researchers can report back to them (Boxes 7.5–7.7), as part of carefully planned and respectful exchanges throughout the project.

Box 7.5   Respect throughout the research

Adrienne Katz, Director of Youthworks Consulting Ltd, founder and former Executive Director of Young Voice

We aim to cooperate with young people as our equals and our consultants. We involve young people from the first planning stage of the research, alongside specialist agencies, professionals and policy makers. Surveys are piloted with young people before use.

We will go anywhere to interview young people, as long as it is safe and reasonable for them and our researchers. We always provide refreshments and travel costs for them. To protect privacy in our research with parents who are young offenders and prisoners, we try to send a different researcher to talk to each member in the same family/relationship, such as a young man, his girl-friend and his mother. The researchers then do not have inside knowledge before meeting interviewees. We use pseudonyms and other disguises in our reports so that relatives will not recognize one another, when we might damage relationships inadvertently.

We protect their identities from the media, and structure confidentiality so that even if schools or police ask us, for example, who has said they use illegal drugs, we do not have the records. Names and personal details are kept separate from

---

all the other data. (We have used a borough's ballot boxes to prevent teachers reading people's replies to our surveys in schools.)

We represent young people's views in our findings and reports. Recent films feature young people and carry the messages from the research. Young people present our research findings at seminars, unless this breaches confidentiality. We always struggle to improve these principles and will not work with partners who won't observe them. (And see also Chapter 9 and Box 9.1.)

Box 7.6   Children and smoking: participant validations

Beth Milton

Towards the end of my longitudinal PhD research on smoking (see Box 8.5), I presented an age-appropriate summary of my findings to focus groups of the 11-year-old participants so that they could discuss and validate the findings. I was very impressed by their thoughtful discussions and reflections on whether the findings were a valid interpretation of the data. Several important themes from these discussions were added to, and greatly enriched, my analysis. I would really encourage other researchers to use participant validation.

Box 7.7   Validations to inform the final report on 'children's experiences of their urban environments'

The researcher and each class discussed a short early report of the findings. The children talked about whether their views were represented fairly and accurately, and about their sometimes strongly expressed views that were missing from the report (in one case, difficult relationships between pupils and teachers). They wanted to know how the research would be used, and their discussion informed the final report (Morrow, 2001).

Reporting back and saying goodbye

Boxes 7.6–7.7 describe ways of validating findings with young people, reporting back to them and drawing what may have been quite close relationships to an end.

Box 7.8   Reporting and reflecting

During the long-term research, Young Lives researchers report back regularly to the communities, who are eager to know what happens to the information they provide. Preliminary findings are presented in accessible ways during meetings, highlighting the usefulness of the data the people are providing. Further information is given, for example, about nutrition in Peru, and about local services in Ethiopia. Researchers also explain how the team is taking messages from the research to governments and advocating for change. However, this raises questions about the likelihood of governments or local policymakers taking notice of research findings and, in the case of longitudinal research, about the time taken for research findings to work their way into policy. In some countries, while families positively support the research, they mistrust the government and feel abandoned by it, and are suspicious of claims that the research will help to relieve poverty (Ames, 2009).

Some of the children recognise that the research encourages reflection. In India, one boy commented about group discussions: I have not seen ... children meeting together and discussing matters till now, no one has discussed like this with children. We feel happy that the researchers are mingling with us. Earlier we never spoke up before anybody. But now we are able to speak out in front of people like you without fear, and this helped us in having courage... we come to know how to speak with elders. (Vennam and Komanduri, 2009: 5, and see Nyambedha, 2008, p. 95)

Researchers can send individual brief printed reports or emails to all participants, or return to discuss the findings with them, or send wall charts of the findings to display in classrooms, corridors or youth clubs. The charts can include pie and bar charts, with short notes about the key findings from the school, and in larger studies alongside them the overall results from all the schools or other groups in the project. Researchers who hold conferences or press launches about their reports may invite participants to attend, and sometimes to give a formal talk.

A main purpose for sharing information early on is to ensure that people are able to give valid informed consent or refusal, the topic of the next section.

Summary of questions

- Are the children and adults concerned given details about the purpose and nature of the research, the methods and timing, and the possible benefits, harms and outcomes?
- If the research is about testing two or more services or products are these explained as clearly and fully as possible?

- Are the research concepts, such as 'consent', explained clearly?
- Are children given a clearly-written sheet or leaflet to keep, in their first language?
- Does a researcher also explain the study and encourage them to ask questions, working with an interpreter if necessary?
- Does the leaflet give the names and address of the research team?
- How can children contact a researcher if they wish to comment, question or complain?
- If children are not informed, how is this justified?

Eight

Consent

Respect for consent has been a theme throughout Chapters 1–7. The careful planning of research, and the ways of informing and communicating with children and young people all lead up to the question about whether they will take part. This is the time for them to decide, and for researchers to stand back, wait and listen.

This chapter reviews the meanings of 'consent', the legal bases for respecting competent children's consent, and the consent of people with parental responsibility. We discuss methods of assessing children's competence, levels of their involvement in decision making, and methods and reasons for requesting and respecting children's consent.

Consent and rights

In Chapter 7 we reviewed how giving information relates to children's UNCRC rights. Informing children and parents is often confused with the different stage of asking for their consent. Respect for their consent or refusal observes the following UNCRC rights: freedom of thought and conscience (Article 14) and listening to children's views (Article 12). When parents decide for the youngest children and guide and support older ones, they fulfil the parental rights and duties 'to provide direction to the child ... in a manner consistent with the evolving capacities of the child' (Articles 14 and 5) and they should be able to further 'the best interests of the child' (Articles 3 and 18). Giving due respect for consent and refusal prevents discrimination against disadvantaged groups (Article 2), the risks of abuse and exploitation (Articles 19, 32, 36 and 37), unlawful interference with privacy and attacks on the child's honour and reputation (Article 17, and discussed further in Chapter 10). Beazley et al. (2009: 370) also draw on articles of the UNCRC to suggest that children have a right to be 'properly researched' (citing Articles 12, 13, 36 and 3), and suggest that 'In research terms this translates into: children being participants in research, using methods that make it easy for them to express their opinions, views and experiences and being protected from harm.'

Most writing about consent involves consent to medical treatment and research. We suggest that the same values of respect, trust, clear information and good communication apply to any kind of consent. Ethical research takes participants' consent, their informed and freely given 'yes' or 'no', very seriously. When adequately informed, young people can clearly understand the point of the consent process and the freedom to say 'no' – if necessary.

One reason to support a common standard of consent is that there is no single measure of low-risk-simple versus high-risk-complex research. To some children, a small study that aims to keep an adventure playground open may be as important, or sensitive, or worrying, as a trial to test a medicine could be. Some small studies can be just as invasive or disrespectful as some large ones.

The meaning of consent

Consent has a tragic history (see Boxes 1.4 and 1.5), which helps to explain the following meanings of consent.

- Consent is the central act in ethics. Valid consent is properly informed (WMA, 1964/2008) and also freely given – without pressures such as coercion, threats or persuasion (*Nuremberg Code*, 1947).
- Respect for people's consent or refusal helps to prevent harm and abuse, such as their feeling deceived, exploited, shamed or otherwise wronged by social researchers.
- Researchers and participants may define 'harm' very differently, and the consent process is the time to clarify any differences. Researchers might gain new insights into risks, and perhaps how to reduce them.
- Potential participants then decide if it is worth taking part in the research despite any risks and costs.
- This process may sound rather extreme for a decision to take part in a small study, but respect for consent sets standards of respect for the whole relationship between the researchers and participants.
- Consent has an impact on all other rights. It is about selecting options and personal preferences, negotiating, accepting or rejecting them. Beyond choosing, consent involves deciding and becoming committed to the decision.
- Much research about consent assesses how people recall and recount the information they were given (Hastings Center, 2002), so it is really about information rather than consent. Instead of being informed, consent is the invisible activity of evaluating information and making a decision, and the visible act of signifying the decision. Consent may be implied, such as by taking part in an interview or survey. Consultations and social research depend on participants' active co-operation, such as to answer questions, and this could be taken as implied consent. People may, however, be afraid, or too embarrassed, to say 'no', unless they are given a respectful chance to refuse, withdraw, or agree to take part in some or all parts of the research.
- In any research, there should be a time for people to be able to ask further questions, to decide, and to say 'yes' or 'no'. Consent may be spoken, or written on a consent form. Researchers may audio record oral consent. Participants should have a copy of the consent form and the information leaflet to keep. There could be a

space on the form for both parent and child to sign, though some children prefer to give oral but not written consent (Alderson, 2007a).

- Consent may be 'one-off' to a single event. For longer studies, such as repeated observations, longitudinal or action research, or trials (including medical trials), or even during an interview or questionnaire, people have the right to change their mind, to withdraw, or to answer some questions but not others. This right should be made clear to them.

Consent to open-ended research

While we were collecting examples for this book, some researchers argued that during open-ended exploratory or ethnographic research, informed consent is not possible, when researchers themselves do not know at first what directions the research might take. However, instead of limiting the respect for participants, which informed consent entails, open research and inquiry can increase such respect. Researchers can work more fully with participants than is possible in tightly pre-planned research, by keeping them informed about, and also centrally involved in, the broad and changing directions, the process of narrowing down the inquiry, and of selecting the later main topics and questions. Researchers may involve many participants, a selected range or a smaller advisory group.

Assent

Guidance often mentions children's 'assent', and there is a large literature especially in the USA, in which it is assumed that children cannot usually give legally valid consent until they are aged 18 or 19, unless they count as 'mature minors'. Authors and guidance in the USA and the European Commission tend to assume that 'children cannot consent' (EC, 2001; Miller, 2004a; NIH, 2007). Ross (2006: 87) states, 'in pediatric research, informed consent includes two components: parents' permission and the child's assent'. Ross (2006: 88) adds that in the USA, permission and assent 'can be waived for minimal risk research' if the waiver will not adversely affect the rights and welfare of the subjects, the research could not practically be carried out without the waiver and whenever appropriate subjects will be provided with additional pertinent information after participation. In other words covert research without consent is allowed in the USA, as it is, for example, in British social research guidance (BSA, 2002; BPS, 2009), although researchers are warned only to waive consent if they think it is essential to their research. The USA guidance illustrates the problem of vaguely assuming that all children can only assent, such a weak version of consent that it can be waived or overridden 'if the intervention or procedure involved in the research holds out a prospect of direct benefit that is ... available only in the context of the research' (DHHS, 1991, CFR s46, 408a; FDA, 1997, Ross, 2006: 220–35). This rule confuses providing a service, which is being researched, with the separate research processes of collecting, analysing and reporting data, see later section on double standards.

We have not used the term assent for three reasons. First, assent refers to agreement by minors who have no legal right to consent. However, English law, which influences the 54 Commonwealth countries, is unusual in the *Gillick* (1985) ruling. Mrs Gillick, a mother of 10 children, sued her health authority in an attempt to ensure that the authority would not provide (contraceptive) medical care or advice to her children aged under 16 years without her knowledge or consent. Eventually, the judges ruled against Mrs Gillick and she now lends her name to a concept with which she disagrees: the *Gillick* competent minor aged under 16 years who can give legally valid consent. The judges did not specifically exclude any child as too young to be *Gillick* competent. Children, therefore, who can make informed, 'wise' and *Gillick* competent decisions are giving consent/refusal rather than assent. Second, assent refers to agreement by children who understand some but not all the main issues required for consent. We question whether a partly informed decision can count as a decision at all, or should have what could be a spurious quasi-legal status such as assent. Third, assent can mean 'at least not refusing'. But that can be very different from actually assenting, such as when children are too afraid, confused or ignored to refuse. Again the term 'assent' may be misused to cover over children's refusal.

Consent and the law

Healthcare researchers and many social researchers are required by RECs/IRBs to state that they have read the *Declaration of Helsinki* (WMA, 1964/2009) and agree to abide by those standards. National and Professional Association Research Ethics Guidelines around the world tend to be based on the *Helsinki* standards of informed consent. In the UK, for example, government guidance (DH, 2005: 2.2.3) states that consent is at the heart of ethical research, and it requires 'appropriate arrangements' for obtaining consent and the review of those arrangements by an ethics committee for health and social research funded by the Department (see also across Europe: EC, 2001; DH, 2004 20/EC). Brazier and Cave (2007: 422–5) are surprised that the European guidance on clinical trials and the COREC (2001: 9,17c) guidance for RECs are 'silent about the consent arrangements for children'. Outside clinical trials there is more respect for *Gillick* competent children (RCPCH, 2000; MRC, 2004). There is no law in Britain about consent to research on human beings, unlike research on animals, foetuses or cadavers, although politicians have required COREC (2006) to issue guidance that strongly supports informed consent to healthcare research. So the law relies heavily on (living) people to protect themselves, in health and more so in social research, by their personal (or parental) consent or refusal.

There are also indirect legal pressures: the Human Rights Act 1998, and law on negligence (not informing participants enough about risks) and assault (touching people without their consent, which applies to medical rather than social research). Although no law compels researchers to observe ethics guidelines on consent, there are other pressures on researchers to do so, which include conditions set by their funders, their employers, their professional associations and organisations (such as education and social services), which grant researchers' access to participants (see References at end of book).

If by any chance researchers were sued, the courts would want to know that reasonable ethical standards had been met. So the ethics guidelines that set out these standards have quasi-legal status. If there is doubt that consent to the research is valid, a signed consent form would be necessary, but not sufficient, evidence. Researchers would also have to show that they gave clear, full information and respected the person's freely made decision.

Research ethics committees, schools and even publishers are now asking to have copies of every signed consent form. However this can break promises of privacy, anonymity and confidentiality. Children who know that people in authority will see who took part in the research are more likely to be identified and to be wary of saying as much as they might like to. Authorities' wish to have copies of consent forms is more to do with protecting them, than respecting children. One of us was told by a large medical ethics committee that we must send them copies of all consent forms. We refused explaining that it would break confidentiality and after some discussion the committee accepted the refusal.

Informed consent is specific, not a blanket general consent 'to anything else the research might involve' (*Code of Practice*, 1990). Researchers should explain everything that they ask people to consent to. If the research plans are uncertain at first, researchers should say so. If the plans change, for example if new topics and questions are added, these should be explained and consent to the new plans should be requested. Medical RECs may require researchers to reapply for approval of such changes.

Consent by and for children and young people

The above points apply to children and young people, and to parents when they decide for or with their children. There are some differences between consent for and by children and adults. This section is mainly about English law, which also influences law in over 50 British Commonwealth countries.

- Adults have greater freedom to take risks for themselves. Choices made by and for children have to be in their best interests (*Gillick*, 1985) or at least not against their interests (RCPCH, 1992/2000).

- In English law, minors over the age of 16 can give legally valid consent to medical treatment (Family Law Reform Act 1969). Competent minors aged under 16 years can also give valid consent. Competence is defined as having 'sufficient under-standing and intelligence to understand what is proposed' and 'sufficient discretion to enable [a child] to make a wise choice in his or her own interests' (*Gillick*, 1985: 423). Since 1985, the 'retreat from *Gillick*' has undermined respect for competent children. Yet the child's consent to medical treatment can override the parents' refusal (*In re* R, 1991; *in re* W, 1992).

- Several experts have advised that *Gillick* applies to many other areas of law beyond medical care – and during the early 1990s they criticised the court cases that undermined the *Gillick* ruling.

- When children are competent, 'As a matter of law the parental right to determine whether or not their minor child below the age of 16 will have medical treatment terminates' (*Gillick*, 1985: 423). Judges see parents as having responsibilities rather than rights, and these are 'dwindling rights' as the child matures (Denning, 1970: 369).

- One statute law, which respects children's decision making, states that when children are capable of consenting to an application to see their health records, parents may only apply with the consent of the child (Access to Health Records Act 1990, s4.2).

- The only people who can give legally valid consent for interventions on children are the competent child and people with parental responsibility – parents, and for looked after children the local authority or the High Court (Children Act, England and Wales 1989). Teachers are *in loco parentis* but do not have parental respon-sibility. They can grant researchers access to children, but cannot consent to the research.

- If doctors were sued by parents or other authorities for respecting a child's consent, they can defend themselves legally by claiming that in their clinical judgement the child is competent (Age of Legal Capacity Act, Scotland 1991). Other professions are unlikely to have this power, which probably only covers treatment and not research.

- English medical research guidelines advise researchers to ask for parents' consent for minors aged under 18 years (RCPCH, 1992/2000; BMA, 2001; MRC, 2004); but they also emphasise that the young child's refusal to take part in research must be respected (RCPCH, 1992/2000).

- The European ruling on clinical trials ignores minors' consent and relies wholly on parents'/guardians' proxy consent (EC, 2001). Children must be informed and their refusal be 'considered' but not their consent. Directives are incorporated into each Member State's national law, to be legally binding. In England, the Directive was extended to cover all medical research (DH, 2004), although this contradicts English case law on minors' consent (Biggs, 2009b).

Double standards

This section is mainly about medical rather than social research, because underlying problems that can complicate social research have been more clearly analysed in medical research. As the previous section showed, there is a double standard. With medical treatment, the child's consent can override parents' refusal, and the parents' consent can override the child's refusal (*In re R*, 1991). But with medical research, the guidance favoured at least until 2004, dual consent from both minors aged under 18 years and their parents, and advised that the refusal even of very young children to take part in research must be respected and might override the parents' consent (RCP, 1990; RCPCH, 1992/2000; BMA, 2001).

Unfortunately, law and debate on consent to research are confused by the mistaken concept of 'therapeutic research' or research that can 'benefit' the child, and this mistake often creeps into social research too. Research means collecting, analysing and reporting data, and cannot directly benefit partici-pants. Research might examine treatments intended to benefit but it cannot be assumed that they will do so: relative benefit is the topic being researched; the treatment may prove to be useless or harmful; children may be in placebo arms or for other reasons not receive a treatment in clinical trials. ('Placebo' means a dummy treatment being compared with real treatments, and each 'arm' is a group having a different intervention in comparative or randomised controlled trials.)

Law and guidance that either advise dispensing with parents' consent, or overriding children's refusal because the research will 'benefit' them are in error and it is more logical to have a single standard for all research, whether or not it tests treatments that might offer benefit (Alderson, 2007a).

An example of 'beneficial' research that can be harmful and misleading is trials with children with asthma. Many children use inhalers daily, to prevent rather than treat asthma attacks. If they stop using inhalers, they are likely to react for days or weeks by having more attacks. If the children take part in randomised controlled trials, they may be in a treatment arm, or in a placebo arm, having dummy or non-treatment. If they have more asthma attacks, they will not know whether this is a reaction to their usual treatment being with-drawn, or to a new treatment being tested, when they are in a double blind trial (when neither patients nor doctors know which arm they are in). Logic, ethics and concern for the children's safety, would suggest that the best trials compare a new treatment against a known treatment, unless there is not yet an accepted treatment, however, in the case of asthma there are many. It also seems obviously unscientific to compare the effectiveness of a drug against non-treatment of a group of children who are having severe withdrawal reac-tions after their usual medication is suddenly withheld. Surely that would give an unfair misleading advantage to the new drug. However, the Food and Drug Administration (FDA), the US agency responsible for medical research, pre-fers placebo trials (Ross, 2006). British ethical guidance (RCPCH, 1992/2000) insists that children should be involved in medical research only if the research cannot equally well be done on adults, and if the findings are intended to ben-efit children. US guidance does not have this standard, so that children are recruited simply to increase numbers of subjects in trials, but with no guarantee that they will be studied as a separate group in order to benefit future child patients (Ross, 2006). Despite bioethics safeguards, harmful and fraudulent medical research and practices continue to be reported (Sharav, 2003; Coppock, 2005; Baughman, 2007; Slesser and Qureshi, 2009), such as the use of dangerous experimental drugs on African children (Save the Children, 2007).

The contrary themes running throughout this book are, on the one hand, ways of preventing and reducing harms in research and ensuring adequate protection of children and young people. On the other hand, is the concern about the risks and harms of silencing and excluding children from research about them and about their views, experiences, needs and participation. We suggest that at present systems do not ensure either adequate protection from harmful or useless research, or adequate participation by children in research that could promote their interests. New attention to children's consent and refusal might help to raise standards, as we review in the rest of this chapter and in Chapter 11.

Complications in parental consent

Parental consent is usually thought to be necessary unless researchers can show that the risks are small enough to rely on children's consent alone. If a case came to court, in which parents and children disagree about research, no one is sure whether the courts would support a child who wanted either to consent or to refuse against their parents' wishes. Yet only a very risky or controversial example would be likely to reach the courts, in which case researches would be wise to ask parents too. For some social research, the *Gillick* ruling about respecting the consent of competent children could surely apply, but this standard has not been clearly or formally agreed.

Researchers, in schools for example, may find it hard to insist on requesting parents' and young people's consent, when they depend on the goodwill of the school. Teachers may say that it takes too much time, expense or delay to ask parents, or even to ask young people, who might refuse or not reply.

To rely on parent's consent can be a vital protection, but it can pose two main problems. One is when parents are informed and they refuse to allow their child to take part although the child is keen to do so (Skelton, 2008). The other problem is when young people have to refuse because they do not want their parents to know that they are using clinical or counselling services, for example, for sexual health, drug, alcohol or self-harm problems (Skelton, 2008).

As Roger Hart and Gerison Lansdown suggest, 'Adults remain the major barrier to effective participation by children' (2002: 10). However, they add that, with parents, this might be because parents are so often bypassed instead of being informed and involved that, if they are asked, they are likely to give negative replies.

> At a minimum, this means that the chance to involve those [parents] who have the greatest impact on children's daily lives [and who can speak for and with children] is lost. But it can have the more damaging impact of creating a struggle of values at home, leading to a backlash against children's rights because parents do not understand them. Sometimes, children suffer punishment for their involvement. (2002: 10)

It can be harder for parents who feel disrespected to respect their children. Ethical research involves informing and respecting everyone concerned. If parents refuse, this is a chance for researchers to exchange better information with them. However, parents may be right to refuse, and ignoring them can remove protections and advocates for children.

Box 8.1   Parental consent: flexible approaches

Will the consent of one parent alone suffice, especially if they live apart? There is no law that both parents must be asked. In a study about separated families, the researchers usually asked the residential parent. They aimed to ask both parents when a child lived part-time with each parent or saw them both often. Yet this could be impossible and intrusive, so the researchers worked with the preference of the child and one parent on how the other parent would be informed and involved or not. The children were adept at moving between separated households and contexts, and an individual flexible approach, tailored to children's real lives and relationships seemed to be the most ethical one (Smart et al., 2001).

Defining and assessing competence to consent

Capacity or competence to consent involves:

- having the capacity to make a choice in relation to a particular proposed treatment;
- knowing the risks, benefits, alternatives;
- understanding that consent is 'voluntary and continuing permission' (DH, 1990: 15.9);
- knowing that consent 'can be withdrawn at any time' (DH, 1990: 15.12);
- each [person] being informed 'fully, frankly, and truthfully' (DH, 1990: 15.11); with 'reasonable care and skill' (DH, 1990: 15.13).

Assessing competence

Competence can be assessed in three ways (Brazier and Cave, 2007: 125–6):

- By status – groups such as adults or very young children.
- By function – through tests of reasoning or other ability.

- By outcome – if the person makes a choice, which the assessor believes will lead to a reasonable outcome, competence is assumed.

The three ways, especially outcome, depend on the assessor's personal views. The manner of testing is important. A highly competent child, who is afraid or angry about being assessed, could appear to be incompetent by not co-operating.

Function tests usually assess four standards in the person giving consent:

- Mental competence, the ability to understand and decide.
- Being sufficiently informed.
- Having sufficient understanding of the case to make a reasoned choice.
- Voluntariness, having the autonomy to make firm personal decisions based on long-term values.

The standards tend to link to *factors specific to each child*, such as, age, gender, ethnicity, ability, maturity and personal experience. Adults may also consider children's hopes, fears, values, life-plans, temperament and degree of independence, and assertiveness and willingness to take risks.

Yet it is equally vital to consider *factors around the child*. Are children usually encouraged to share knowledge and decisions or not? Are they used to being listened to? What is the research setting like, welcoming or intimidating? What research is being discussed, how complex is it? Have the children been told all the main points (listed in Boxes 2.1, 7.1–4 and 8.2)? These look daunting but can be condensed into clear short leaflets (see Chapter 7). If children and parents are to be well informed there may be barriers to overcome. These include finding enough time and a quiet space to talk, people who are skilful and confident about sharing information, overcoming language barriers, using simple words, and responding to children's cues and body language.

The function tests will then also involve assessing the concerned adults.

- Are they competently helping the child to understand and decide?
- Are they sufficiently informed and skilled in explaining the information?
- Do they have sufficient understanding to make a reasoned choice and to understand the reasoning of the child's choice?
- Do they respect children who have competence and autonomy?

A hospital chaplain and former head teacher thought that respecting children's decisions involved transferring power from adults to children, and needed courage and maturity in both adults and children. As an adult, 'Am I big enough to say, "Whatever you choose will be valued … I'll do all I can to support you and we'll go forward together"? It's such a big step for the adult to surrender power to the child' (Alderson, 1993: 143). A study about special education also found that some young children's decisions are taken seriously (Box 8.2).

Box 8.2   Respecting a child's choices in education

Susan is blind and she insisted on moving from her local school, when four-years-old, where she felt 'smothered and mothered', to be a weekly boarder at a special school. When she was aged ten, she recalled when she was four how, 'Mum had to drag me screaming down the [school] drive because I didn't want to go home.' Susan visited several secondary schools and eventually decided to board at her present school and attend a nearby public school. 'It would be a struggle but I would get the hang of it,' she decided. Her father explained her choice to the local authority, which agreed to grant the funds. A year later, Susan was very pleased with her decision, academically and socially. In some ways, only Susan could make a fully informed decision that took account of her experiences, values and plans (Alderson and Goodey, 1998: 119–20).

As adults, before we can begin to respect children's views and consent, we have to rethink how and why children are often seen as untrustworthy. Important research, conducted over 20 years ago, about children as witnesses in court has shown that they can distinguish reality from fantasy (King and Yuille, 1987). Even pre-school children, and children with learning difficulties can be reliable witnesses, and can recall and reconstruct central events accurately, when they are carefully questioned, treated considerately and have a 'support person' present (Murray, 1988). 'A child should be presumed to be a competent witness, unless there is good reason to reach a different conclusion' (Murray, 1988: 82).

It is hard to demonstrate competence, and easier to spot incompetence. For this reason, it is better to start from a presumption that the (school age) child is competent when talking with children about the research and their views (RCPCH, 1992/2000; BMA, 2001). The term 'participants' gains real meaning when adults and children become partners in all stages of the research including consent and checking competence together, to protect and respect the child. This means checking the child's ability and also the adults' skill to help the child to understand as much as possible. In terms of Box 8.3, the aim is to move from view 1 to include view 2 as well.

Box 8.3   Two views of consent

View 1	View 2
Legal contract	Negotiation
Event	Process
Facts	Awareness
Static knowledge	Growing knowledge
One-way	Two-way exchange of information
Testing the child	Enabling the child

Levels of involvement in decision making

A problem with consent law is that it is all or nothing. It concerns competent people or parental consent, but says nothing about non-competent people's rights. However, the UNCRC, for example, clearly sets out levels (1–3, below) that respect all children (and see Chapter 3). The levels are:

(1) To be informed.
(2) To form and express views.
(3) To influence a decision.
(4) To be the main decider about proposed treatment or care (Alderson and Montgomery, 1996).

In English law, *Gillick* goes beyond the UNCRC to the fourth level. Most children and many adults prefer to stop at level 3 and to share serious decision making with people close to them. Yet at any age it can be very distressing to feel forced into a decision against your will. Very young children are able to form views and to understand simple explanations, and so they may be competent at level 4.

Degrees of respect for children

Ladders show different levels of involving children, from superficial manipulation of the ignorant child and tokenism, through children being assigned to tasks or decisions but not informed. Next is the level of children being consulted and informed, and finally the levels (of participatory research) when children are willing and able to share and initiate decisions (Hart, 1992).

Respecting consent and refusal

To help children and parents to give informed and unpressured consent or refusal, they should be told about their rights.

- Consent means being able to yes or no.
- People should have time to decide.
- There will be no pressure on them while they decide.
- They are welcome to ask questions and discuss their views with a researcher.
- They may wish to talk to a friend or other person before they decide.
- They can refuse or drop out at any time without needing to give a reason.

To ensure participants are aware of their right to drop out, researchers can remind them later, ask if they are happy to carry on and tell them that if they do that it will not affect any care or service they are having that is linked to the research. They will still get the best possible care.

Information leaflets (see Chapter 7) can also make these points in the following ways.

Asking for consent:

- Will you help us with our research?
- Will you take part in an interview and fill in three questionnaires?
- Will you help us to try out the new maths course?
- Are you interested in being in a documentary about students who are excluded from school?

Box 8.4   Explaining rights

Do I have to say yes?

No. It is up to you whether you take part in this research. No one should feel forced to agree. You do not have to give a reason for saying 'no', although giving a reason might help the research.

Before you agree, you need to feel sure that the research is worthwhile. If you are not sure what to decide, take time to think. You may want to talk to other people before you decide.

You may also change your mind, and withdraw from the study at any time. Please tell us if you do so, but again you do not have to say why.

When the research is linked to a service such as teaching or social work, which the child is already receiving: If you refuse or withdraw we shall still give you the best care/teaching/services that we can.

It is vital to avoid coercion, especially when potential participants may be multiply disadvantaged in, for example, being children, having few reading skills, speaking another first language, being unused to making and defending a refusal, or saying 'no' to adults, who are strangers and who belong to a more powerful group, one that might provide resources for the child and family. The Young Lives (2006: 11) fieldworker instruction handbook states:

Staff should not pressurise, coerce or deceive respondents in an effort to ensure their participation. Staff should also try to ensure that respondents are not pressurised by other family or community members ... The respondents will have at least 24 hours to consider whether they want to take part and will be free to withdraw from the study at any time.

As noted in Chapter 7, researchers are asked to carefully explain to children in ways they can understand, why they are there. It points out that children are generally taught from a very young age that they must obey adults, making it difficult for them to refuse researchers. So it must be made clear that there will be no adverse consequences for them if they refuse to take part.

Box 8.5   Consent and young people who do not use speech

In one study, the young people used a mechanical breathing aid and could not talk. They used a technical communication aid or other methods. Some had carers who interpreted their facial expressions and gestures. Some used home-made alphabet boards. Their carers pointed to each letter until the correct one was reached, and gradually each word was spelt out. The young people were able to give informed consent using these methods. Interviews were lengthy and tiring, so they were held over two visits. How could the young people's views be conveyed vividly when they could not give verbatim quotes? A young art student of about the same age listened to the scenarios the young people had described, and drew cartoons about them. One showed how carers may unnecessarily restrict the lives of the young people. When shown the cartoons, the participants said they felt the cartoons powerfully portrayed their views and experiences (Noyes, 1999).

Box 8.6   Children and smoking: assent and whole-class research

Beth Milton on her PhD research

My multi-method school-based longitudinal study of 250 children's experiences of smoking when aged 9–11 used questionnaires, draw and write with whole classes, focus groups and interviews. To ensure that children could refuse or opt-out, I used three protective layers of permission (head teachers, parents and children's assent). However, assent was a problem in the classrooms. Many children did not want to draw and write, but their teacher insisted that they did

(Continued)

(Continued)

the exercise, and gave sweets to everyone to ensure compliance. As a visitor in the classroom I could not overrule the teacher, and I also felt compromised by my desire to collect data from each child. In whole class research, there needs to be provision for some children to refuse, perhaps to go to another room, though this would be hard to achieve in many schools. This raises ethical issues, as assent should be genuine with a real opportunity to opt-out, but this often clashes with the usual power relationships between teachers and pupils, especially when teachers value 100% participation.

Consent to longitudinal research

Some research involves long-term follow-up, historical and longitudinal review, through continuing use of research data. This may be done by the research team or by other researchers. If follow ups might be done later, should researchers ask people to agree at the start of the research, or towards the end of the first wave of the research?

Longitudinal research may last weeks, months, years, even decades over a whole lifetime, as in the big English birth cohort studies of people born in 1958, 1970 and 2000. As they grow older, children gradually become more informed and able to make their own decisions about whether to confirm or to end the consent arrangement given at first by their parents, and they should have the chance to do this at each renewed research contact.

Consent to answer questions is fairly simple compared with the next complication: consent to the primary data being stored for later use by other research teams for secondary analysis, and for as yet unknown future purposes. 'Consent' might here be so broad and vague that it cannot really be consent; it is certainly not informed. There are risks that their data (meaning 'given things') will be used in ways that the donors would disagree with and not wish to support.

A further complication is when researchers and RECs consider that secondary analysis does not raise ethical questions because there is no direct contact with participants and therefore no risk of harming them. Some researchers describe their work as 'secondary analysis', when it is primary except in so far as other teams collected the data, partly because they claim they do not need REC approval. This means that research is regulated by neither consent nor RECs, and it is even more crucial that RECs have some oversight. Considerable harm can be done through primary and secondary analysis, research reports, dissemination, media reports, and influences on policy, practice and public opinion (see Chapters 9 and 10).

Box 8.7   Repeated permission and consent

Young Lives research teams (Morrow, 2009) attempted to ensure reasonably that equal minimum standards of informed consent were met in all four countries, in the following ways:

- Research teams initially approached community leaders and then individual parents and children (in most countries researchers have to work past several 'gatekeepers' before meeting the children).
- Enumerators and fieldworkers sought and recorded informed consent from parents and children at the beginning of each visit, and each session or activity, and ideally again at the end of the session in relation to how the data would be used, or agreement to participation in future activities.
- Researchers provided contact details of the research teams and detailed leaflets that they read out to ensure minimum standards of information.
- Some teams found that signing a paper consent form was not acceptable for various reasons, mostly because people were wary of putting their signature on forms, so they voice-recorded oral consent with the digital recordings being stored (but not transcribed).
- Other teams have found it inappropriate to use voice-recorders, but record the consent process in their field notes. Consent is understood to be an ongoing process. A fieldworker in Vietnam noted that 'local people ask lots of questions about us as researchers and the research, and we always take time to answer their questions and to obtain their views about the research'.

During the Young Lives study, one older Ethiopian boy refused to participate, despite his parents' willingness for him to do so. 'There was some speculation ... that the boy had heard a rumour from his friends that Young Lives has a mission to convert children to Protestantism' (Tafere et al., 2009: 9). This demonstrates differences in views between parents and children, though of course parents may have had similar fears. That children's views about participation are respected must be understood positively as informed consent operating in practice. Further, those who refuse on one visit may consent during the next visit, and might agree to discuss their previous refusal.

In Young Lives, research relationships have to be sustained over a long period of time, and requests for informed consent have to be renewed.

Consent and secondary data analysis

Primary research teams may involve secondary data analyst teams directly, or they may archive their data for other researchers to access and use for their own purposes. This can complicate consent. Do researchers ask potential participants before they enter the study to consent to secondary use? This can risk boring and confusing people, overloading the informed consent process and increasing refusal rates. Alternatively asking later in the project for agreement to secondary data analysis can risk people feeling deceived or betrayed that they were unable to give adequately informed consent at the start and that they will lose confidentiality. Some people might feel they would have provided data differently, more cautiously perhaps, if they had known in advance. Or they might worry about potential uses, which they could disagree with or even oppose. Researchers can partly respond to the latter concern by requiring all potential secondary data users to explain their plans and obtain the primary researchers' approval before they can have access.

Longitudinal data are often presented in graphs and grids and as separate variables, which conceal participants' identity. The next example is more complicated of modeling detailed qualitative case studies over ten years of 100 young people's transition to adulthood.

Box 8.8   The amplified ethical problems of secondary analysis of qualitative longitudinal research

Rachel Thomson and colleagues, Open and South Bank Universities, UK, Inventing Adulthoods Study 1996–2006

When the study began, we had no plans to archive the data or to continue for ten years. Gradually as the years went by and we managed to continue, we saw that to realise the full potential of the data set we would have to build a community of secondary analysts. Ethical problems of secondary qualitative data analysis involve recreating context, the role of the primary researcher, and protecting participants. Repeated interview encounters over the years become more than the sum of their parts. Seeming inconsistencies and contradictions begin to make sense and to open deep insights into the individual's psyche. We offered participants a copy of their tape after the third session, to help them to be able to give more informed consent each time it was renegotiated. Each of the 100 case histories became more complex and easily identifiable, although we changed names and key identifying details, and I wanted to consult each person before deciding to publish their own case. Karin, for example, said she found reading her records 'cringe-worthy'. Although she thought they were accurate, she was surprised to be reminded of some of her past thoughts. She thought it would have been easier not to see the record and that she would be more wary and self-conscious in future interviews.

We try to ensure that our interventions in the young people's lives are as benevolent as possible and aim to balance realising and doing justice to the potential of the data with concern for the well-being of the participants (Thomson, 2007, 2008; McLeod and Thomson, 2009).

Researchers are finding ways of explaining data archiving in ways that are understandable and locally relevant. The example in Box 8.9 is from Young Lives.

Box 8.9   Explaining data archives

Young Lives research teams explain what archiving is, and reassure participants about anonymity, and disguising identifying features (of places, people, organisations) in preparing data for archiving. For example, in Peru, the term 'un archivo' is understood, since almost all villages and communities own archives with documentation regarding the village, which is for public consultation. India suggested 'stored in a computer'. In Vietnam, researchers note:

> We used the word 'storage' (pack and store away), pointing to a cupboard or wardrobe or trunk if any of those are available in the house, or simply a box or a bag. Since we brought our laptop to the field, children saw us typing notes. We showed them what we typed – excerpts of transcripts of what they said (even if some can't read) – and pictures (of their house, no person). We also replayed a short part of the tape to that they could hear their voice. We then explained that all of these will be kept in Hanoi and England for many years but nobody will know that these words are theirs or go after the children because of what they have said. The children and their family members were quite excited, some were scared at first, then became very proud (see also Goodenough et al., 2003; Helgesson, 2005).

International standards of consent

The Pfizer trial in Nigeria illustrates the potential importance of consent.[1] In 1996, during a big meningitis epidemic, which killed 11,000 people, Pfizer tested an antibiotic in the slum city Kano, saying it was a 'humanitarian mission'. Critics said it was an unlicensed medical trial. Near the Pfizer clinic, Médecins Sans Frontières was also dispensing medicines.

Pfizer selected 200 children, half were given a routine antibiotic and half were given the experimental one, Trovan. Eleven of the children died and many more, it is alleged, later suffered serious side-effects ranging from organ failure to brain damage. 'But with meningitis, cholera and measles still raging and crowds still queuing at the fence of the camp, the Pfizer team packed up after two weeks and left.' About 18 months later, 'a Pfizer employee, Juan Walterspiel wrote to the then chief executive of the company, William Steere, saying that the trial had "violated ethical rules". Mr Walterspiel was fired a day later for reasons "unrelated" to the letter, insists Pfizer. The company claims that only five children died after taking Trovan and six died after receiving injections of the certified drug Rocephin.' They also claimed that the meningitis, not their drug trial, harmed the children.

> But did the parents know that they were offering their children up for an experimental medical trial?
>
> 'No,' Nigerian parent Malam Musa Zango said. He claims his son Sumaila, who was then 12 years old, was left deaf and mute after taking part in the trial. But Pfizer has denied this and says consent had been given by the Nigerian state and the families of those treated. It produced a letter of permission from a Kano ethics committee. The letter turned out to have been backdated and the committee set up a year after the original medical trial.
>
> At one time Pfizer faced the prospect of an US$8 billion fine and imprisonment for several staff. In April 2009, Pfizer settled out of court to pay £50 million, although the case may continue. The drug Trovan is no longer produced. It has been banned in the EU and withdrawn from sale in the USA.[1]

An initial response might be: social research could never have these kinds of harms and risks. However, we suggest that although they may be less immediate and visible, some social, educational and economic interventions can damage people's lives. Standards change and what might seem minor routine decisions at the time can later turn out to have unexpected momentous effects. And if it is agreed that medical researchers should meet high standards, should not social researchers meet them too?

The Pfizer example also questions the criticism that 'Western' ideas of consent are too individualistic, and misunderstand other notions of community. When a child dies or is seriously disabled and needs lifelong care, becoming a burden on the family instead of a resource and contributor, the effects of research are imprinted on the individual child's mind and body and on the closest carers' daily life and relationships. Instead of individuals being blurred and lost within the group, the medical research example illustrates the strong impact each individual can have in closely knit groups, perhaps even more so when families lack statutory social welfare supports and have to provide all the extra care and resources themselves.

Research in international contexts

This section reviews some conventional guidance, which might be qualified by the Pfizer and other similar examples. Differing cultures may have very different views on and approaches to 'informed consent'. The ESRC Research Ethics Framework (2005) recognises that, in developing countries:

---

[1]http://www.independent.co.uk/news/world/africa/pfizer-to-pay-16350m-after-deaths-of-nigerian-children-in-drug-trial-experiment-1663402.html (accessed 24 February 2010).

The conventional meaning of informed consent may be problematic because the conventional model of consent rests on 'the primacy of the individual'. The individual is seen as both the owner of rights and the bearer of reciprocal duties to the rights of others. This emphasis on the individual can seem inappropriate or meaningless in some cultural contexts, where the individual may take less precedence than broader notions of kin or community. (ESRC, 2005: 24; see also Brown et al., 2004)

There is a danger here of a false dichotomy between 'majority' and 'minority' world countries in relation to ethics. First, the emphasis on the individual might seem inappropriate in some cultural contexts, but when something goes wrong and children are damaged, the focus will rightly be drawn to the individual. Second, in the minority world too, children are seldom seen as completely separate persons, but as sons, daughters, brothers, sisters, friends, members of families and other communities. However, we need to consider ways in which children and childhood are understood in local contexts (Ennew and Plateau, 2004; Laws and Mann, 2004; Schenk and Williamson, 2005; Ahsan, 2009).

Afua Twum-Danso (2009) reports how children in group discussions in Ghana said that they rarely challenged adult authority, and that they preferred to be told what to do. Otherwise they risked being seen as deviant and disrespectful, being punished and insulted (as witches or devils), and they brought shame on their parents. 'If you do not express your opinion you do not die', some children commented, saying that they rated much more highly rights that would help them to survive. Twum-Danso comments that this belief assumes secure parental care. However, increasing numbers of parents are abandoning their responsibilities to their children. She observed that despite the children's claims, in practice they often actually behaved to the contrary and many said they could exchange intimate views frankly with their mothers.

Caroline Gokonyo, reporting her qualitative research about a malaria vaccine trial in Kenya, states, 'Individual informed consent is a key ethical obligation for clinical studies, but empirical studies show that key requirements are often not met' (2008: 708). The ways to strengthen consent in low-income settings include seeking permission from community members through existing structures before approaching individuals, considering informed consent as a process not an event and assessing people's understanding using questionnaires. Gokonyo's study found all these approaches were valuable and the team gave information on several occasions before requesting consent. She discovered that interpersonal relationships and trust between researchers and communities critically influenced participants' decisions to consent, refuse or withdraw as well as their evaluations to the researchers at the end of the trial. These approaches are well beyond the timescale and the reach of most studies, but researchers are expected to meet increasingly ambitious, stringent, formal standards for informed consent. Gokonyo concludes that the formal standards need to be counterbalanced with greater respect and attention to the diverse, complex, often unpredictable and ever shifting social relationships and ethical dilemmas facing researchers 'in the field'.

The problems encountered during the consent process can help researchers to become more aware of the related complex standards, relationships and interactions, and then to work towards more effective ways of meeting conventional models and local preferences. Gokonyo's finding about consent decisions being based on the quality of the relationship applies across the world. Ethnographic research about parents' consent to children's heart surgery found personal, emotional and moral relationships affected the parents' views (Alderson, 1990).

Why respect children's consent?

Respect is a basic ethical principle. Listening to children can help adults to discuss and resolve children's misunderstandings. This can reduce the coercion of resisting or resentful children, and the risk of complaints. Transparent discussion can encourage consent as informed willing commitment by children and young people to a research study that they understand. Their active co-operation and contributions are then likely to support more efficient and effective research. They are less likely to withdraw from a study. Researchers may gain vital knowledge from children about ways to improve the research.

As mentioned earlier, some guidance permits covert research (BSA, 2002; BPS, 2009). We suggest that this relies on old unethical views and methods that treat research subjects as ignorant objects. The new psychology guidance (BPS, 2009) still does not expect REC review to be routine, which makes the individual's right to consent or refuse an even more necessary protection. Mention that their consent should be requested after the data gathering has taken place misunderstands the true meaning of consent as a free choice with the right to refuse. Researchers who respect children's consent and feel accountable to them are more likely to take their views seriously throughout the research.

We also suggest that informed partnerships, when researchers have to explain and be accountable for their plans and methods, are more likely to improve the research aims, theories and methods, than covert approaches can do. Research findings, and conclusions too, may be more accurate when discussed openly with children and young people, such as about their own motives even for their deviant or criminal activities. In the next example, researchers could have drawn misleading adult-centred conclusions if they had not consulted the children as partners (Box 8.10). This small example shows the value of explicit over covert research.

Box 8.10   The book corner

Researchers showed children photographs of each main area of their early years centre, and asked them which area they liked best and least. The book corner was the least popular. Might this mean the children were immature? Was it a signal to improve the books or the corner? During discussions, the children said they disliked the way the corner was used. They had to sit there quietly when the staff were busy. They became bored when sitting in a large story group that did not interest everyone. So the staff changed the ways they used the corner and arranged the story groups (Miller, 1998).

Clear information leaflets for children can also help parents, who may not have fluent reading skills or use of English, to make more informed decisions about whether their child should be invited to take part in research. Leaflets can reduce the risks of parents feeling confused, uncertain and perhaps intimidated into permitting dubious research on children, and can help parents to know how to support children during the research.

Researchers who do not respect children's consent or refusal may well hold and perpetuate mistaken and unethical prejudices against children. Realistic research that respects children's social and moral competence challenges prejudices, misleading stereotypes and harmful discrimination. It helps to promote ethical standards of respect and justice.

Ethics guidance tends to emphasise consent during the data collection stages of research, but the later stages when research findings are disseminated and influence society also have important effects on children, which researchers could address when requesting consent. These are the topics of the next two chapters.

General questions about children's consent

Several problems about consent cannot be resolved by individual researchers alone. These include:

- Can and should researchers sometimes ask only for children's and not for parents' consent in addition?
- How can children's competence be assessed in ways that convince critics that children's competence and consent are genuine?
- Should there be different standards for consent to medical versus social research, or to academic research versus consultations and evaluations, or for research conducted by young people, by students or by adults?

These questions are also considered in Chapter 11.

Summary of questions

- As soon as they are old enough to understand, are children told that they can consent or refuse to take part in the research?
- Do they know that they can ask questions, perhaps talk to other people, and ask for time before they decide whether to consent?
- Do they know that if they refuse or withdraw from the research this will not be held against them in any way?
- How do the researchers help the children to know these things, and not to feel under pressure to give consent?
- How do they respect children who are too shy or upset to express their views freely?
- Are parents or guardians asked to give consent?
- What should researchers do if a child is keen to volunteer but the parents refuse?
- Is the consent written, oral or implied?
- If consent is given informally, how do the researchers ensure that each child's views are expressed and respected?
- If children are not asked for their consent, how is this justified?

PART 3

The writing, reporting and follow-up stages

Nine

Disseminating and implementing the findings

This book follows questions about ethics as they arise through the stages of research. Chapters 1–8 were concerned about early planning, and also about setting standards for every stage of the research. Instead of writing separate chapters about the data collection and writing up stages, we leave readers to draw on Chapters 1–8 for questions that arise in these mid-project stages. Justice and respect are key themes while you decide how to select, present and interpret the items in your reports. We now move on to the end-of-research and after-project stages.

This chapter considers the meaning of dissemination and how it goes beyond writing reports and books. Research with and by children and young people offers exciting dissemination opportunities. These include exhibitions of children's art and design, photographs and videos, and public presentations of their research through lectures, poems, games and drama, at meetings ranging from local to international, and on radio, television, the internet, and in the public press.

Do people have an ethical duty to try to make their research findings widely known and, if possible, acted on? Dissemination involves publicity and public debates about research, and we review some ethical questions about dissemination through a range of methods and media. We also look at methods for critical readers to use, before they decide whether to disseminate other people's research findings by supporting them or applying them through their own work.

Involving children in data analysis

Involving children in the interpretation and analysis of data may be perceived as being difficult (Mayall, 1994), but increasingly researchers are trying to do this. One of us attempted to involve children in analysis of data they had produced by reporting some preliminary findings (in research about young people's 'social capital', their friendships and communities) in an oral presentation (Morrow, 2008). I gave children a leaflet outlining the main themes I had identified, and that I planned to analyse in more depth (see Morrow [2008] for the leaflet). Children were asked whether they felt their views were being represented fairly and accurately. In group discussions, I was challenged – quite rightly – by one student, who pointed out that I had failed to include an adequate analysis of what had been discussed about the (poor quality of) relationships between teachers and children. By focusing on children's views of their neighbourhoods, I had missed the point that schools are important communities from children's point of view, as sources of social relationships, and friendships, as well as sources of (sometimes) difficult encounters with adults. My subsequent analysis addressed this much more carefully than if I had not reported back my preliminary analysis to the children concerned.

Coad and Evans (2008) discuss practical approaches to involving children in data analysis, drawing on research they conducted – in one case involving children aged 10–16 in a study of a proposed purpose-built children's unit in a new hospital. Children acted as an advisory group to the project, and were involved in analysing data from interviews that were then used to construct a questionnaire for children. Children were also involved as peer researchers. Coad and Evans emphasise that involving children in data analysis takes time and resources, children (like adults working in teams) need time 'to get to know each other, [to] develop relationships of trust and gain the confidence and skills' to undertake data analysis (2008: 50). There are also ethics questions to consider, (but these are the same as for adults) about confidentiality, anonymity, and dealing with distressing questions that might relate to their own difficulties.

Dissemination: getting to the heart of debate and change

A published research report may only reach very few people. Dissemination, however, means sowing seeds, and is more widespread and has deeper effects than publication alone. Research studies with children often raise emotive, political and ethical debates because, openly or not, they are concerned with inequalities between adults and children, and whether these are fair and beneficial. So the seeds, the ideas that are spread around by research findings, are not simply thoughts for people's minds. They may also involve deeply felt beliefs. Research studies that aim to sow the seeds of change in policies, services or beliefs about children and young people have to involve people at a thinking and also a feeling level, which can challenge and upset some of them. Debates during dissemination, like the other stages of research, also concern tensions between promoting children's participation and also protecting them.

Dissemination and implementation: children, young people and adults working together for change

During many research studies, there is little time to write reports, let alone to discuss the findings at conferences and other meetings with people who plan policies and work with children. One way round this problem is to include these activities as a central part of the funded research, involving children and young people, and experienced practical adults from the start. Box 9.1 gives an example from India, Box 9.2 is about Liverpool, UK, and disabled young people, the Children's Society and university researchers. Box 9.3. is an example from London.

Box 9.1   Implementing research in India

P.J. Lolichen (2007: 251), who works with The Concerned for Working Children, Bangalore, describes an innovative study conducted by children aged 9–18 about transport and mobility in their communities in Karnataka, India. The children identified the questions to be studied, and conducted the research themselves. They collected and documented the information, and have disseminated their findings and 'are working with various stakeholders in the communities to address the problems identified, such as building or fixing footbridges, starting crèches, filling potholes, blacktopping roads. They are also negotiating with the key stakeholders such as the gram panchayat, the school authorities, and others to institutionalise children's participation in their panchayat.'

Box 9.2   Disabled children and young people and the local council

The Disability and Diversity group project in Liverpool promoted continuous service planning, decisions and delivery, shared between the local authority and agencies and disabled young people. They moved away from short consultations and quick fixes, and advised on services such as integration, advocacy, transition, reviews, packages of care and responding to complaints. Through forums, newsletters, IT networks and advocacy they developed agreed standards and a culture that promotes and values young people's participation, building on young people's own agendas and communication methods. Deaf children chose to join in because a British Sign Language interpreter they knew

(Continued)

(Continued)

was involved. About 40 people aged 9–21 took part in group discussions, conducted by people aged 16–21 years.

The group raised £150,000 for inclusive creative projects: an art and drama project; peer education/counselling; disability equality training for staff and students in schools; independent advocacy and support across local services, and access checks on local buildings and events. They ran apprenticeships for disabled young people to become access auditors. They achieved more equal power relationships and partnerships between adults and young disabled people. The project shows how active, imaginative and creative they were despite shortages of time and funds, besides the challenges of inclusive work with young and disabled people, and hidden dangers in altering power relations through participatory projects. Serious work on changing society must be mixed with creativity and fun, to stop 'participatory' projects from oppressing young people (Davis and Hogan, 2004).

Box 9.3   Children's views of London

The Office of Children's Rights Commissioner for London based its work on the UNCRC. Young people trained others about their rights and how to participate politically in important ways, such as their active involvement in London Assembly meetings. Their large survey conducted with nearly 3000 young Londoners identified their major problems with poverty, racism, housing, schools, health, transport and environmental planning, and lack of good resources and services for young people, Additionally it considered ways for young people and adults to work together to prevent the causes of crime (OCRCL, 2001, 2002a, 2002b). Their work led the Mayor of London (2004) to agree to develop the city-wide Children's Strategy with and for children and young people and to commission the *State of London's Children* reviews (Hood 2002, 2004) based on children's priorities.

Problems with dissemination

Many difficulties can obstruct dissemination and here we list a range of numbered and paired problems then solutions.

(1)   Funders or other authorities may stop reports from being published.
(2)   People may dismiss reports saying that they are weak or distorted.
(3)   Dissemination can involve months or years of working with policymakers and practitioners, at conferences and other meetings, on how to link research findings

and conclusions into their work. Few researchers have the time or funding to do this.

(4) Links between the research evidence, and the report, and what they mean for policy and practice are often not clear. Many researchers then prefer to leave practical experts to work out the links. Yet few of these experts have the time or interest to read long research reports and to do the often difficult connecting work. The reports then may remain unused.

(5) People may misunderstand and misapply the findings of research or consultation.

(6) The mass media can be very helpful with dissemination, but they may present over-simple, sensational or inaccurate reports.

(7) Busy people have so much to read, that they prefer short clear reports. It is often hard to report complex detailed research in short simple terms.

(8) The research may not be worth disseminating. It may repeat other work, or be unfinished or unconvincing.

(9) Editors may refuse to publish the research if it is unethical, such as by being conducted without consent, or if they think a report is poorly written or boring. The findings may be unpopular, or disbelieved, or attacked and dismissed.

Creative ways round the problems

Here are some suggested solutions linked to the numbered problems above.

(1) Include a right-to-publish clause in the research contract or agreement with funders and employers (see Chapter 5).

(2) Ask critical friends to check research reports and revise the report to answer their criticisms.

(3) Include funds, time and, possibly, training, to enable researchers to publish their work for different relevant groups, including short reports for the children and parents, for professionals and policymakers working with and for them, and for popular magazines or television programmes they are likely to see.

(4) Researchers and practical experts can learn much from one another when they discuss how to link research to policy and practice, and researchers may then be able to write more relevant and practical reports. These discussions can be valuable extra stages of research studies to recognise and fund, especially now that there is more concern about the impact of research. Further research may be planned. One example of such is the current rapid change in policies about children's rights and participation, from national government to small local group levels. The changes were promoted by NGOs' practical research projects and publicity about children's rights.

(5) When researchers take part in professional, policy and public debates about their research, this helps to increase other people's understanding and use of their findings. And the debates may help researchers to see how to make their reports more convincing and readable.

(6) News media/journalists often over-simplify and distort their versions of research reports. However, you might find an informed journalist who supports children's interests and rights to write about your research. We suggest that problems with the media are too complex for individuals alone to resolve, as we will discuss later.

(7)   Reports written at different levels and lengths, academic, practical and popular, reach more readers. Writing short reports for research participants helps researchers to analyse and sum up their work clearly. See the Rowntree website (www.jrf.org.uk) for examples of *Findings*, clear four-page summaries. Page 1 lists about six key points, pages 2–3 explain each point, and page 4 gives a few details about the researchers, and the methods and outcomes. *Findings* are backed up by longer reports, so that readers can choose their reading level depending on their interest. Abstracts at the start of journal articles offer another layered approach. Abstracts are far more widely read and quoted than the full papers, especially those on websites. Their accuracy is therefore very important.

(8)   The problem of research studies that do not produce reports worth publishing shows the importance of careful planning of the research aims, methods, timetable and ethics from the start. Reports need to be clear and transparent about the methods and about any limitations of the study. For example, it is important in small-scale research not to over-generalise from the findings. A study of 50 young carers cannot claim that 'all young carers tend to be depressed' even if all those in the study happen to say that they are sometimes depressed. Large samples are not needed when reporting exceptions, which refute generalisations. For example, only a few examples of skilful or informed young children can challenge assumptions that no children at their age can be so competent.

(9)   Research findings that are surprising, counter-intuitive, and genuinely challenge or refute popular views can make vital contributions to knowledge, to theory, evidence, policy and practice. Yet they may be the hardest kind to get acceptance from reviewers and editors and be published, and may suffer from unfair criticism.

Dissemination and news media

As already mentioned, the news media can be very helpful – and sometimes very unhelpful – when publicising research. Journalists tend to ask for personal stories, and want to film and talk to children and young people who took part in the study. This raises problems about confidentiality (Chapter 3). Young people are often keen to be in the news, but researchers must be wary of risks if children can identify themselves in public reports, or be identified by others. The problems include children feeling very upset or angry by the way they have been portrayed, being teased and derided, losing friends, or attracting unwanted publicity to themselves, to their group or school. Strangers may contact them, and exploit, threaten or even harm them. The research ethics of respecting privacy and personal reputation and safety may be forgotten.

Conversely, children and young people may enjoy the publicity, feel very pleased about their success, and perhaps achieve the policy changes they aim for with the help of media support. Positive news stories made with and about young people help to challenge generally negative stories and images.

The CRAE (2009b) report *Another Perspective* explains how journalists can promote children's rights and equality by respecting children on an equal level with adults. Journalists often denigrate children in ways they would not dream of treating Black, disabled or other minority adult groups. The report shows how investigative and campaigning journalists can report injustices, acknowledge progress, promote positive image work with campaign groups, make space for news and analysis about children that investigate context and go beyond superficial stories, take care over images and their portrayal of childhood, work with children and young people, take account of their best interests and report in ways to interest and inform younger readers. The report has lists of useful sources and contacts (CRAE, 2009b).

Box 9.4   Working positively with the media

Adrienne Katz, YoungVoice

We try to work with the media to produce fair and respectful reports – a complex and difficult aim. It is impossible to 'control' the media, but these approaches help.

- Choose your target journalists by following their work over time. Avoid intrusive or sensationalist ones. Be clear with them about your way of working, such as confidentiality. The Samaritans (2008) have good media practice guidelines.
- If young people in your research study want to do media work, and a journalist wants to speak to them, check with them first, then give them the journalist's telephone number (if you approve of that person!). Never give the journalist the young people's numbers. For people under 16, get their parents' permission too. Be clear that they can withdraw and are not doing it just to please you.
- Discuss their rights with the young people. They may be able to insist on seeing journalists' drafts. Do they realise that they might be misquoted? Should they keep a record of what they say? You could offer to go with them to the interview, though not to sit in on the session.
- We thank young people who do media work for us by taking them to a restaurant, for example, or for a shopping trip with vouchers, or a sightseeing trip in London. Then we can offer them support after their interview. We often give them a thank you voucher for their time, or their drawings or photographs.
- We supply newspapers with photos that we own all the rights to. All young models in our photographs have signed a form of consent to various uses of this image. Parents also sign along with people aged under 16. We try to negotiate fees for young people who do interviews or supply their photos to journalists. (And see Box 7.5 on always holding personal details in separate files from all other data, so that identified individuals' replies can never be given to the police or anyone else.)

Critical readers and viewers

This final section reviews how policymakers, people working with children and young people, and journalists interpret and apply research findings. Their responses vitally affect how research is generally understood and used. Box 9.5 lists methods for critical readers to use, when deciding which ideas from reports to accept and apply, and thereby to disseminate through their work.

Box 9.5   Ethical questions for critical readers

Is the reported research effective and not a waste of time and resources? For example:

- Does the research method fit the aims and questions, and connect these clearly to the findings and conclusions?
- Are the links well argued?
- Do the samples or cases provide enough evidence to support the conclusions?
- What models of childhood and youth do the authors explain or imply that they hold? Respectful, realistic, positive or negative?
- Do the researchers treat the young people as research objects, or participants, or co-researchers?
- How do the researchers say they thought about and tried to resolve any ethical problems?
- What do they say about consent?
- Do they thank the young people who helped with the research in their reports?

Underlying attitudes to children and the 3 Ps

Children's rights can be divided into the '3 Ps': Protecting or Providing for children, or encouraging children and young people to Participate, such as by expressing their own views and contributing to their families and communities. The 3 Ps partly overlap and are often complementary but carry different emphases. Which of the 3 Ps do the authors emphasise, through the topics, methods and findings of the research? Authors' views of children's three kinds of rights can test how they see and relate to children:

- as victims or problems who need Protection and control;
- as dependents in need of services and other Provision;
- or as Participants who share in partnerships when defining and solving problems.

Chapter 10 continues the theme of dissemination by looking at the impact that publicity and the use of research can have on children and young people.

Summary of questions

- Does the research design allow enough time to report and publicise the research?
- Do the reports show the balance and range of evidence?
- Will the children and adults involved be sent short reports of the main findings?
- Will the research be reported in popular as well as academic and practitioner journals, so that the knowledge gained is shared more fairly through society?
- Can conferences or media reports also be arranged to increase public information, and so to encourage the public to believe that it is worthwhile to support research?
- Will the researchers meet practitioners to talk with them about practical ways of using the research findings?

Ten

The impact on children

Most ethics guidance is concerned with the personal cost and benefit to participants during the data collecting stage (Chapter 2). Much less is said about the ethics of the likely impact of the published reports, either on children in the study or on related groups of children and young people. How might they stand to gain or lose? Research can affect very large numbers of children, beyond the individual researcher–child relationship, when influencing public and media opinion and professional policy and practice. For example, do research reports about teenage parents or street children increase respect and practical support for them, or increase prejudice against them? Although researchers cannot wholly control the way their findings are used, they can select the issues they examine, the questions and methods, the ways they interpret their findings and the terms they use.

This chapter reviews the social context of research with children and young people, the collective impact that research reports can have on them, and the sometimes unintended effects. We consider what it means to share power with children and young people, and we end by reviewing the use of positive images.

All social research and consultations have political aspects, such as examining how equally knowledge, resources and control are shared. Traditional work on the family that seemed neutral has been shown to be adult-centred. When researchers look specifically at the children rather than the whole family unit they find, for example, that children rarely have an equal share of space and resources at home, or in society. Whereas many old people have several rooms to themselves, young children tend to live in homes with less than one room per person (Gordon et al., 2000; Hood, 2004). Debates about ethical research involve reviewing how research reveals instead of conceals such inequalities between adults and children (see earlier chapters, specifically Chapter 4).

What collective impact can research have on children and young people?

The impact of research includes both the effects on young research participants during a study, and also the longer-term effects that findings might have on attitudes and policies about all similar children and young people, and services for them. The effects may or may not be intended.

One example is medical research charities' use of images in advertising. Until recently, images of sickly thin children were used to raise funds for research about cystic fibrosis. Thanks to medical research, most children with CF no longer look thin or sickly, and many expect to live well into middle age. Young people with CF were unhappy that public stereotypes stopped people from seeing them as lively individuals and as potential employees, mortgage holders and partners. It is counter-productive when funds for medical research are raised through negative slogans and images, which endorse the attitudes that hold young people back from fully enjoying the benefits that the research now confers.

Another example concerns research with teenage parents, which continues to find that many of them manage very well, despite problems arising from stigma and hostility towards them (Carter and Coleman, 2006).

Media reports about young asylum seekers tend to be hostile, with occasional pity for their plight and their treatment in detention centres. Tense racial relationships between adults in communities are often reported, whereas little is heard about the closer relationships British young people and young asylum seekers are able to form in schools. Groups of school students have protested when their asylum seeking friends were sentenced to be detained and then deported, and some have managed to get the sentences revoked and the young people returned to school (Pinson et al., 2010). Researchers who hope to publicise such positive examples widely, and to inform public opinion, face double and treble prejudices when their findings are about young people, about disadvantaged groups, and about ethnic and religious minorities. Few journalists report research about this kind of success and solidarity, examine how problems can arise from social attitudes and policies or analyse young people's own reasons for their activities. Many researchers therefore feel wary about reporting their work with children in the media in case it is presented unfairly. This question, of whether to keep quiet, or to risk being misreported in ways that could harm young people, is one that researchers can hardly resolve individually (though see Box 9.3 and Chapter 11).

Another problem is when research reports have little or no impact. Implementation takes time and is complex. Researchers who involve children and young people and report their views tend to have little influence. A review of participation projects with children and young people found that very few of their imaginative and creative ideas were implemented (Willow et al., 2004; and see Percy-Smith and Thomas, 2009). 'Children and young people have been giving the same key messages to decision makers for several years, and … despite this, there is little evidence of [any] impact on the development of strategic plans in the major service areas of health, education and social services' (Donnelly, 2003: 3; and see Kirby et al., 2003).

Reviewing the impact of research on children

Leading questions for ethical review about how research affects children are:

- What will the planned and possible impact of the research reports be on children and young people, those in the study or in related groups?
- And, in some cases, should the research be done at all?

Governments have to report to the UN Committee on the Rights of the Child every five years on their progress in implementing all aspects of the UNCRC (all reports and the Committee's responses are on www2.ohchr.org). In many countries, the NGOs working for children present parallel, and usually much more critical, five yearly and also annual reports (for the UK see www.crae.org.uk). Perhaps a similar overview or audit report could be made regularly on research and consultation with and about children and young people. It could cover:

- the main areas, disciplines and agencies concerned;
- sources and amount of funding;
- research on matters that affect children but which took account only of adults' interests, activities and views;
- issues important to children that are not researched;
- methods and values in research about and/or with children;
- who gave consent;
- involvement of children and young people in any of the stages of the research from planning to implementation;
- general trends in the data and conclusions that have positive, neutral or negative emphases;
- links or lack of links with policy and practice, and the responses of policy makers;
- news media publicity about the research;
- how the research promotes positive or negative views of childhood and youth.

Even if only a few of the largest social funders and research centres produced such reports, the findings could help future ethics and policy reviews and planning.

When research does have lasting effects, children may be influenced by the resulting policy changes in three ways.

- The policies may immediately affect children now.
- They may affect children in future when they are adults and see the impact on their own children.
- The effects may last into the far future when today's children are old, long after the researchers have gone.

These three ways entitle children to have even greater share in helping to plan current research and future policies.

Positive images

From the mid-1990s, leading NGOs have aimed to use positive pictures, such as during famine appeals they publish images of active children collecting water instead of helpless starving babies. They have promoted respect for children's dignity through images that avoid stereotypes, and sentimental or demeaning pictures of dependency that do harm as well as good. This positive policy can also apply to research, in its topics and themes, headings, questions, and the language and tone of its reports. Campaigns to reduce derogatory stigma and to increase respect, originally from women's and disability movements and from Black Pride campaigns have transformed public attitudes and language. Much remains to be achieved with children and young people, who are routinely denigrated in public (yobs), in ways that would be unthinkable for other minority groups. Equal opportunity standards to eradicate prejudice, discrimination and negative stereotyping involve aiming to include and respect all groups of children and young people at every stage of research from first plans to final publicity. Chapter 11 will sum up practical points raised through the book to suggest future policy.

Summary of questions

- Besides the effects of the research on the children involved, how might the conclusions affect the larger groups of children?
- What models of childhood are assumed in the research? Children as weak, vulnerable and dependent on adults? As immature, irrational and unreliable? As capable of being mature moral agents? As consumers?
- How do these models affect the methods of collecting and analysing data?
- Is the research reflexive, in that researchers critically discuss their own prejudices?
- Do they try to draw conclusions from the evidence, or use the data to support their views?
- Do they aim to use positive images in reports, and avoid stigmatising, discriminatory terms?
- Do they try to listen to children and to report them on children's own terms though aware that children can only speak in public through channels designed by adults?
- Do they try to balance impartial research with respect for children's worth and dignity?

Eleven

Conclusion

Since the first two versions of this book were published in 1995 and 2004, there has been very welcome growth in the following areas:

- research and consultation directly with and by children;
- the reporting of children's own views and experiences;
- the range of methods used with and by children;
- the valuable lessons from research by NGOs and with children in other continents;
- respect for children's rights and participation;
- formal research ethics committees and ethics training for social research, and
- concern about ethics in social research and consultation.

We look forward to perhaps even greater changes over the next 15 years.

Ways forward for individuals and teams

We suggest that in future these trends are encouraged and developed further.

- Growing understanding among researchers about the use of ethical questions and standards in every aspect of research.
- Willingness to raise ethical research standards through seeing the advantages, rather than through fear about the risks of ignoring the standards.
- An increase in participatory research with children, when the ethics of justice and respect for rights, the methods and the outcomes, all reinforce one another.
- Public, media and policy attention for research about children's competence, making for more informed, respectful and inclusive communities.
- Concern for the impact on children during research, and to plan new standards based on respect for children.
- Greater concern from policymakers and people working with children and young people to apply the findings of ethical research and consultations.

Questions that cannot be solved by individuals alone

Most of the above points can be achieved by individuals and research teams working alone. However, if certain further questions are to be addressed adequately, researchers need support from higher authorities. These questions, some of which have been raised earlier, include:

- When can we rely solely on children's consent and not have to ask for the parents' consent as well?
- Can we involve children who consent, if their parents refuse?
- Are there fairly simple agreed methods to check whether children are competent to consent to join a research study?
- Should students doing under- and postgraduate degrees be allowed to do research directly with children and young people, given the lack of time for meeting reasonable ethical standards?
- How can respect for children throughout the research process, aims and impacts, be taken more seriously by people who plan, fund and vet the research?
- Can current policies about research and about routine training of students be revised, when these involve covert or distressing methods and negative questionnaires?
- Could funders more routinely support the extra costs of ethical, inclusive projects with children, that prepare and follow up the work with them? And how can funders and researchers promote higher ethical standards in very low-cost short research studies?
- Can double standards, of careful REC review for some research studies and no review for others, be justified?
- Can researchers and journalists work together more to promote accurate and respectful media reports of research with children and young people – just as journalists now avoid racism and sexism?

The need for social research ethics authorities

There are several reasons why individuals and research teams alone cannot answer the above questions. The questions do not have simple answers based on logic and evidence. Instead, they involve values, justice, respect, protection and vested interests. Health researchers now accept that questions of ethics are not decided convincingly either by individuals or by remote elite groups alone, because other groups may challenge them. Researchers cannot, for example, side-step patients' consent simply by saying, 'Trust me I'm a researcher.' To convince critics, they need a general climate of firm support for agreed standards from respected, independent authorities such as RECs and IRBs, supported in Britain by COREC and their Association AREC.

To be credible, RECs acknowledge the sometimes conflicting interests of participants, researchers and research, and they aim to respect the participants' interests first. Attempts to impose ethics standards deny the principle of respect and will only fail. RECs include members from a range of backgrounds who challenge one another. They debate disagreements and negotiate ethical standards among all stakeholders, through compromise and towards consensus. Education and explanation are needed to encourage all concerned to accept and 'own' new standards – in a large-scale version of the consent process with respect for all participants. This is a continuing political process of revising and raising standards and meeting the challenges of new areas of research. These include new collaborations, such as inter-national and inter-disciplinary research projects; new topics, from genomics and biobanks to the views of the youngest children; new research media such as websites and chat rooms.

Health care researchers tended to dismiss research ethics 30 years ago, but now they widely regard REC approval as an essential and useful protection. The system can be very flawed (Jaffer and Cameron, 2006) but is generally accepted as better than no system at all. Social researchers are setting up similar systems, in all the universities for example, but might they aim to promote better ones? Social research does not have the generous funds for administration and training paid to medical research ethics by the pharmaceutical firms, but neither does social research have the associated dangers of fraud, which lavish funding fosters. The fairly lax BPS (2009) and BSA (2002) guidelines, which allow covert research and do not require REC review, indicate that social research has some way to go before reaching healthcare research ethics standards.

Summary of national policy

Summarising the points in this section, we suggest that:

- Stronger social research ethics authorities are needed, to promote higher standards.
- The authorities need to be, and to be seen as being, reasonably independent and impartial, such as by including a range of stake holders and outsiders or really independent 'lay' people.
- They have to work through negotiation and consensus, through explanation and education, so that those concerned gradually come to 'own' and consent to, or at least accept, the agreed standards.
- The authorities can be essential ethical mediators in the very unequal relationship between researchers and research subjects.
- They help researchers to be accountable and to recognise and aim to meet ethical standards.

Some social RECs are working on these activities. We conclude by proposing that their work could be clarified, consolidated and strengthened by a national forum for social research ethics. The forum would:

- Cover all the main disciplines and professions in social research.
- Include representatives from leading funders and commissioners, professional associations, and from government, voluntary, academic and commercial research agencies.
- Involve research participants, adults and young people, as independent 'lay' members, and preferably have a 'lay' chair.

- Involve experts on ethical and legal matters.
- Have adequate funding.
- Agree and periodically review and revise national guidance through wide consultation.
- Promote meetings, training, courses and debates about social research ethics.
- Promote efficient networks of local RECs.
- Approve which kinds of social research and consultation, if any, need not go through REC review.
- Advise on difficult questions that local RECs cannot resolve.
- Work with national agencies, such as government and the mass media, on linking research to policy, practice and public debate.

The forum could perhaps consult at national level with policymakers and service providers about why research repeatedly reports children's and young people's (and many adults') views, but these views are still ignored.

Is the research worth doing?

We began with this central question, which may seem to have been lost at times in the chapters on methods and processes. Yet can research be ethical unless in its content and purpose it is designed to answer worthwhile questions that have not yet been clearly answered? And does worthwhile ethical research also involve respecting children and their rights? This section reviews some current trends in research, and ethical questions they raise for the future.

Support services and management in British universities have greatly expanded and they increase the costs of research, so that researchers now have to raise (or 'capture') grants that include high overheads. These come mainly from government research councils and departments, and now seldom come from the charitable trusts, which have funded more flexible, child-centred innovative research, but do not cover overheads. Increasingly, the large funders are setting the research agenda, questions, methods and purposes, which reflect values in the government's children's policies *Every Child Matters* (HM Treasury et al., 2003). The policies emphasise: the costs of childhood; poverty to be reduced by more parental employment; the risks that children will not fulfil their potential to become high-earning adults but might instead become a drain on health, social or criminal justice services. The agenda could be read as one of defensiveness, wariness and even hostility towards children. There are concerns that US anthropologists are being drawn into military defence (Price, 2008). British international aid and development are being expanded in very complicated ways that complement defence policies (DFID, 2009). It is worth asking if research about childhood and youth is being drawn into slightly similar government defensive anxieties and management, in this case of inter-generational tensions. How does research about child development relate to international development and defence?

Multi-million pound projects – trials, evaluations and cohort studies – are big businesses. They employ many assistants (doing technical data collection, collation and checking), and may sell on their data for secondary analysis, in order to make better use of the wealth of resources, and also to help to cover the huge costs. Here are a few of the questions these trends raise for directors and funders of research in all parts of the world.

- In large numerical data sets and with large hierarchical research teams, how can children's (and junior researchers') views be heard and respected?
- Might economic emphases in the purposes and processes of large projects treat children as cost units of analysis rather than as persons?
- Is there an emphasis on family functioning over the value to children and parents of diverse relationships and experiences? And what are the consequences of pro-moting unduly narrow norms?
- How does the research further children's best interests and present well-being, as well as their future adult potential?
- How does the research investigate children's perspectives using emancipatory par-ticipative methods and positive (rather than negative) questions?
- Is attention to problems within families balanced by concern with economic, politi-cal and social pressures on families? Are politicians' responsibilities for children's wellbeing appropriately addressed?
- What are the implied models of childhood (children as contributors, victims, costs, risks) and how might over-negative models become fatalistic self-fulfilling prophe-cies, for example, about the poorer prospects for disadvantaged children?
- Do evaluations attend sufficiently to positive aspects of childhood and to weak-nesses in services?
- How does the research in its remit and methods promote equity, and address the severe economic and ecological problems and debts facing future generations?

And finally

Throughout this book we have aimed to balance giving attention to the ways to protect children and young people and prevent and reduce harm, with the ways to respect and involve them, listen to them and learn from them, and to avoid silencing and excluding them. We suggest that present systems do not adequately either protect children from harmful and useless research, or pro-mote their participation and their interests. We suggest that most of this book about children also applies to all other research participants, especially disad-vantaged ones. We hope this book will promote local and national debates and action on raising ethical standards in research.

References

This list is mainly of sources cited in the text, although we have included further relevant references to provide for a comprehensive list of resources.

Abebe, T. (2009) 'Multiple methods, complex dilemmas: negotiating socio-ethical spaces in participatory research with disadvantaged children', *Children's Geographies*, 7, 4: 451–465.

ABPI (Association of British Pharmaceutical Industry) (2001) *Current Issues in Paediatric Clinical Trials*. London: ABPI.

Access to Health Records Act S.4. (2) (1990).

Age of Legal Capacity (Scotland) Act S.2.(4) (1991).

Ahsan, M. (2009) 'The potential and challenges of rights-based research with children and young people: experiences from Bangladesh', *Children's Geographies*, 7, 4: 391–403.

Alderson, P. (1990) *Choosing for Children: Parents' Consent to Surgery*. Oxford: Oxford University Press.

Alderson, P. (1993) *Children's Consent to Surgery*. Buckingham: Open University Press.

Alderson, P. (1995) *Listening to Children: Children, Ethics and Social Research*. Barkingside Barnardo's.

Alderson, P. (1998) 'Living with cystic fibrosis', *Association of CF Adults Magazine*, Autumn: 8–9.

Alderson, P. (1999) 'Did children change or the guidelines?', *Bulletin of Medical Ethics*, 150: 38–44.

Alderson, P. (2000) 'Children as researchers', in Christensen, P. and James, A. (eds) *Research with Children*. London: Routledge Falmer, pp. 241–257.

Alderson, P. (2000a) 'School students' views on school councils and daily life at school', *Children and Society*, 14: 121–134.

Alderson, P. (2007a) 'Competent children? Minors' consent to health care treatment and research', *Social Science and Medicine*, 65: 2272–2283.

Alderson, P. (2007b) 'Governance and ethics in health research', in Saks, M. and Alsop, J. (eds) *Researching Health: Qualitative, Quantitative and Mixed Methods*. London: Sage Publications, pp. 283–300.

Alderson, P. and Morrow, V. (2006) 'Multi-disciplinary research ethics review: is it feasible?', *International Journal of Social Research Methodology: Theory and Practice*, 9: 405–441.

Alderson, P. and Goodey, C. (1998) *Enabling Education: Experiences in Ordinary and Special Schools*. London: Tufnell

Alderson, P. and Montgomery, J. (1996) *Health Care Choices: Making Decisions with Children*. London: Institute for Public Policy Research.

Allen, G. (2005) 'Research ethics in a culture of risk', in Farrell, A. (ed.) *Ethical Research with Children*. Buckingham: Open University Press, pp. 15–26.

Alimo, K. and Klug, B. (eds) (2002) *Children as Equals. Exploring the Rights of the Child.* New York: University Press of America, Inc.

Amaya-Jackson, L., Socolar, R., Hunter, W., Runyan, D. and Colindra, R. (2000) 'Directly questioning children and adolescents about mal-treatment', *Journal of Interpersonal Violence*, 15, 7: 725–759.

Ames, P. (2009) 'Peru data gathering report 2008. Second qualitative round of data collection', Young Lives internal document/technical note.

Ansell, N. and Van Blerk, L. (2005) 'Joining the conspiracy? Negotiating ethics and emotions in researching (around) AIDS in Southern Africa', *Ethics, Place and Environment*, 8, 1: 61–82

Armbruster, H. and Laerke, A. (2008) *Taking Sides: Ethics, Politics and Fieldwork in Anthropology.* Oxford: Berghahn Books.

Baughman, F. (2007) *The ADHD Fraud: How Psychiatrists Make Patients of Normal Children.* Victoria BC: Trafford.

Beale, B. and Hillege, S. (2004) 'Impact of in-depth interviews on the interviewer', *Nursing and Health Sciences*, 6: 141–147.

Beauchamp, T. and Childress, J. (2000) *Principles of Biomedical Ethics.* New York: Oxford University Press.

Beazley, H. and Ennew, J. (2006) 'Participatory methods and approaches: tackling the two tyrannies', in Desai, V. and Potter, R. (eds) *Doing Development Research.* London: Sage Publication, pp. 189–199.

Beazley, H., Bessell, S., Ennew, J. and Waterson, R. (2009) 'The right to be properly researched: research with children in a messy, real world', *Children's Geographies*, 7, 4, 365–378.

Bell, M. (2009) *An Invitation to Environmental Sociology. Third Edition.* London: Sage Publications.

Bell, N. (2008) 'Ethics in child research: rights, reason and responsibilities'. *Children's Geographies*, 6, 1: 7–20.

Beresford B. (1997) *Personal Accounts: Involving Disabled Children in Research.* London: The Stationery Office.

Biggs, H. (2009a) *Healthcare Research Ethics and Law.* Abingdon: Routledge.

Biggs, H. (2009b) 'Competent minors and healthcare research: autonomy does not rule, okay?', *Clinical Ethics*, 4, 4: 176–180.

Borland, M., Hill, M., Laybourn, A. and Stafford, A. (2001) *Improving Consultation with Children and Young People in Relevant Aspects of Policy-making and Legislation in Scotland.* Edinburgh: The Scottish Parliament.

BMA (British Medical Association) (2001) *Consent, Rights and Choices in Health Care for Children and Young Pople.* London: BMA.

Boyden, J. and Ennew, J. (eds) (1997) *Children in Focus – a Manual for Participatory Research with Children.* Stockholm: Radda Barnen.

Bradley, B. (1989) *Visions of Infancy.* Cambridge: Polity.

Bray, L. (2007) 'Developing an activity to aid informed assent when interviewing children and young people', *Journal of Research in Nursing*, 12, 5: 447–457.

Brazier, M. and Lobjoit, M. (1991) *Protecting the Vulnerable: Autonomy and Consent in Health Care.* London: Routledge.

Brazier, M. and Cave, E. (2007) *Medicine, Patients and the Law.* London: Penguin.

Bricher, G. (2001) 'If you want to know about it just ask: exploring disabled young people's experiences of health and health care', unpublished PhD thesis, University of South Australia.

BERA (British Education Research Association) (1992*) Ethical Guidelines.* Slough: BERA.

BPS (British Psychological Society) (2007) *Conducting Research on the Internet: Guidelines for Ethics Practice in Psychological Research Online.* Leicester: BPS.

BPS (British Psychological Society) (2009) *Ethical Guidelines and Support: Code of Ethical Conduct*. Leicester: BPS.

Brooker, E. (2002) *Starting School: Young Children Learning Cultures*. Buckingham: Open University Press.

Brunton, G., Harden, A, Rees, R., Kavanagh, J., Oliver S. and Oakley A. (2003) *Children and Physical Activity: A Systematic Review of Barriers and Facilitators*. London: EPPI-Centre, University of London.

BSA (British Sociological Association) (2002) *Guidelines for Good Professional Conduct and Statement of Ethical Practice; Statement of Ethical Practice*. Durham: BSA. Available at: http://www.britsoc.co.uk (accessed 18 February 2010).

Campbell, A. (2007) *An Ethical Approach to Practitioner Research*. Abingdon: Routledge.

Cambridge, P. (1993) 'Taking account of user choice in community care', in Alderson P. (ed.) *Disabled People and Consent to Medical Treatment and Research*. London: Social Science Research Unit, University of London, pp. 28–37.

Candappa, M. (2002) 'Human rights and refugee children in the UK', in Franklin, B. (ed.) *The New Handbook of Children's Rights*. London: RoutledgeFalmer, pp. 223–236.

Carroll-Lind, J., Chapman, J., Gregory, J. and Maxwell, G. (2006) 'The key to gatekeepers', *Child Abuse & Neglect*, 30, 9: 979–989.

Carter, S. and Coleman, L. (2006) *Teenage Parenthood*. Brighton: Trust for Study of Adolescence/Young People in Focus.

Cashmore, J. (2006) 'Ethical issues concerning consent in obtaining children's reports on their experience of violence', *Child Abuse & Neglect*, 30, 9: 969–977.

Children Act (England and Wales) (1989) Part V, 43 (8) London: HMSO.

Chakraborty, K. (2009) '"The good Muslim girl": conducting qualitative participatory research to understand the lives of young Muslim women in the *bustees* of Kolkota', *Children's Geographies*, 7, 4: 421–434.

Cheney, K. (2007) *Pillars of the Nation: Child Citizens and Ugandan National Development*. Chicago, IL: University of Chicago Press.

Children in Scotland (2002) *Research/Consultation Guidelines*. Edinburgh: CiS.

Children's Forum (2002) 'A world fit for us', *Children's Rights Information Network News*, 16: 12.

Christensen, P. and James, A. (eds) (2000) *Research with Children. Perspectives and Practices*. London: RoutledgeFalmer.

Clacherty, G. and Donald, D. (2007) 'Child participation in research: reflections on ethical challenges in the southern African context', *African Journal of AIDS Research*, 6, 2: 147–156.

Clark, A. and Moss, P. (2001) *Listening to Young Children. The Mosaic Approach*. London: National Children's Bureau/Joseph Rowntree Foundation.

Clarke-Jones, L., in Alderson, P., Clarke-Jones, L. and Schaumberg, H. (2002) *Notes Towards an Evaluation of The Office of Children's Rights Commissioner for London: Phase 1. 2000–2001*. London: Social Science Research Unit, University of London.

Cleves School and Alderson P. (ed.) (1999) *Learning and Inclusion: the Cleves School Experience*. London: David Fulton.

Coad, J. and Evans, R. (2008) 'Reflections on practical approaches to involving children and young people in the data analysis process', *Children & Society*, 22, 1: 41–52.

Cockburn, T., Kenny, S. and Webb, M. (1997) *Moss Side Youth Audit: Phase 2, Indicative Findings in Employment and Training*. Manchester: Manchester City Council and Manchester Metropolitan University.

Cocks, A. (2006) 'The ethical maze: finding an inclusive path towards gaining children's agreement to research participation', *Childhood*, 13, 2: 247–266.

Code of Practice Pursuant to Section 118(4) of the Mental Health Act 1983 (1990) London: HMSO.

Cohen, L., Manion, L. and Morrison, K. (2000) *Research Methods in Education*. Abingdon: RoutledgeFalmer.

Cooter, R. (ed.) (1992) *In the Name of the Child: Health and Welfare 1880–1940*. London: Routledge.

Coppock, V. (2005) 'Meeting the challenge? Voicing children and young people in mental health research', in J. Goddard et al. (eds) *The Politics of Childhood*. Basingstoke: Palgrave Macmillan, pp. 245–262.

COREC (2001) *Governance Arrangements for NHS Research Ethics Committees*. London: COREC.

COREC (2006) *Memorandum of Understanding between MHRA, COREC and GTAC*. London: COREC.

Coren, E., Hutchfield, J., Iredale, W. and Thomae, W. (2010) 'Qualitative and quantitative findings from an evaluation of action for Children's National Child Sexual Abuse Services', report to funders. Available on request from esther.coren@canterbury.ac.uk

Coyne, I. (2009) 'Research with children and young people: the issue of parental (proxy) consent', *Children & Society*, 24, 3: 227–237.

Coyne, I., Hayes, E. and Gallagher, P. (2009) 'Research with hospitalised children: ethical, methodological and organisational challenges', *Childhood*, 16, 3: 413–429.

CRAE (2007) *Research Ethics Statement*. London: CRAE.

CRAE (2008a) *Get Ready for Geneva: Children and Young People's Report to the UN Committee on the Rights of the Child*. London: CRAE.

CRAE (2008b) *Full Report of the Child and Young People's Research, get ready for Geneva*. London: CRAE.

CRAE (2008c) *UK Implementation of the UN Convention on the Rights of the Child, England. Alternative Report to the UN Committee on the Rights of the Child*. London: CRAE.

CRAE (2008d) *State of Children's Rights in England*. London: CRAE.

CRAE (2009a) *State of Children's Rights in England*. London: CRAE.

CRAE (2009b) *Another Perspective: How Journalists can Promote Children's Rights and Equality*. London: CRAE.

Curtis, K., Roberts, H., Copperman, J., Downie, A. and Liabo, K. (2004) '"How come I don't get asked no questions?" Researching "hard to reach" children and teenagers', *Child & Family Social Work*, 9, 2: 167–175.

Danby, S. and Farrell, A. (2005) 'Opening the research conversation', in Farrell, A. (ed.) *Ethical Research with Children*. Buckingham: Open University Press, pp. 49–67.

Davis, J. (1998) 'Understanding the meanings of children: a reflexive process', *Children & Society*, 12, 5: 325–335.

Davis, J., Watson, N. and Cunningham Burley, S. (2000) 'Learning the lives of disabled children: developing a reflexive approach', in Christensen, P. and James, A. (eds) *Research with Children*. London: Routledge/Falmer, pp. 201–224.

Davis, J. and Hogan, J. (2003a) *Diversity and Difference Consultation and Involvement of Disabled Children and Young People in Liverpool*. Liverpool Bureau/The Children's Society.

Davis, J. and Hogan, J. (2003b) 'Research with children: ethnography, participation, disability, self-empowerment', paper to ESRC Disability Seminar Series: *From Theory to Practice: Implementing the Social Model of Disability*. Edinburgh: University of Edinburgh.

De Block, L. and Buckingham, D. (2007) *Global Children, Global Media: Migration, Media and Childhood*. London: Palgrave.

Denning LJ in *Hewer v. Bryant* [1970] 1 QB 357, 369.

Dench, S. (2004) 'RESPECT: professional standards in social research', *SRA News*, September.

Denzin, N. and Giardina, M. (2007) *Ethical Futures of Qualitative Research*. San Francisco, CA: Left Coast Publishing.

DfES (Department for Education and Skills) (2001) *Code of Practice Concerning Special Educational Needs*. London: DfES, paras 33: 15–16.

DfES (2001a) *Core Principles for the Involvement of Children and Young People*. London: Children and Young People's Unit.

Department for International Development (2009) *Eliminating World Poverty: Building our Common Future*. London: DFID.

DH (Department of Health) (1990a) *Patient Consent to Examination or Treatment* HC. (90)22.

DH (1990b) *Code of Practice Pursuant to section 118. (4) of the Mental Health Act 1983*. London: DH.

DH (2001a) *Consent – What You Have a Right to Expect: A Guide for Parents*. London: DH.

DH (2001b) *Research Governance Framework for Health and Social Care*. London: DH.

DH (2004) *The Medicines for Human Use Act: Clinical Trials Regulations*. London: DH. Available at: http://www.mhra.gov.uk (accessed 25 July 2010).

DH (2005) *Research Governance Framework for Health and Social Care*, 2nd edn. London: DH.

DHHS (Department of Health and Human Services) (1991) *Code of Federal Regulations*. Washington, DC: DHHS.

Dockett, S., Einarsdóttir, J. and Perry, B. (2009) 'Researching with children: ethical tensions', *Journal of Early Childhood Research*, 7, 3: 283–298.

Dominelli, L. and Holloway, M. (2008) 'Ethics and governance in social work research in the UK', *British Journal of Social Work*, 38, 5: 1009–1024.

Donnelly, M. (2003) *Consulting Children and Young People in Liverpool*. Liverpool: City Council.

Dunn, J. (1998) 'Young children's understanding of other people: evidence from observations within the family', in Woodhead, M., Faulkner, D. and Littleton, K. (eds) *Cultural Worlds of Early Childhood*. London: Routledge, pp. 101–217.

Edwards, A., Sebba, J. and Rickinson, M. (2007) 'Working with users: some implications for educational research', *British Educational Research Journal*, 33, 5: 647–661.

Einarsdóttir, J. (2007) 'Research with children: methodological and ethical challenges', *European Early Childhood Education Research Journal*, 15, 2: 197–211.

Ekstedt, J. and Nomura, B. (2002) 'A place at the top table in South America', *Children's Rights Information Network News*, 16: 15–16.

Emmison, M. and Smith, P. (2000) *Researching the Visual*. London: Sage Publications.

Ennew, J. and Plateau, D. (2004) *How to Research the Physical and Emotional Punishment of Children*. Bangkok: International Save the Children Alliance.

ESRC (Economic and Social Research Council) (1999) 'Children 5–16 Research Programme'. Available at: http://www.hull.ac.uk/children5to16programme/ (accessed 20 February 2004).

ESRC (2005) *Research Ethics Framework*. Swindon: ESRC.

ESRC (2009) *Framework for Research Ethics*. Swindon: ESRC.

EC (European Council) (2001) *Clinical Trials Directive 2001/20/EC*. Brussels: EC.

EU (European Union) (n.d.) RESPECT. Available at: http://www.respectproject.org (accessed 25 July 2010).

Evans, R. and Becker, S. (2009) *Children Caring for Parents with HIV and AIDS: Global Issues and Policy Responses*. Bristol: Policy Press.

Faden, R. and Beauchamp, T. (1986) *A History and Theory of Informed Consent*. New York: Oxford University Press.

Farrell, A. (ed.) (2005) *Ethical Research with Children*. Buckingham: Open University Press.

FDA (Food and Drugs Administration) (1997) *Federal Register*, 62:43900–16.

Finch, J. (1984) '"It's great to have someone to talk to": ethics and politics of interviewing women', in Bell, C. and Roberts, H. (eds) *Social Research: Politics, Problems, Practice.* London: Routledge, pp. 166–180.

Fisher, C. (2003) 'A goodness of fit ethic for child assent to nonbeneficial research', *The American Journal of Bioethics*, 3, 4: 27–28.

France, A. (2000) *Youth Researching Youth: The Triumph and Success Peer Research Project.* Leicester: NGA/JRF.

Franklin, B. (ed.) (2002) *The New Handbook of Children's Rights.* London: RoutledgeFalmer.

Gallagher, M., Haywood, S., Jones, M. and Milne, S. (2009) 'Negotiating informed consent with children in school-based research: a critical review', *Children & Society*, online early view.

Galloway, D., Armstrong, D. and Tomlinson, S. (1994) *The Assessment of Special Educational Needs: Whose Problem?* London: Longman.

Global Humanitarian Forum (2009) *Human Impact Report: Counting the Human Cost of Climate Change.* Geneva: United Nations.

Gibson, F. and Twycross, A. (2007) 'Children's participation in research', *Paediatric Nursing*, 19, 4: 14–17.

Giddens, A. (2009) *The Politics of Climate Change.* Cambridge: Polity.

Gillick v. *West Norfolk and Wisbech AHA* 1985 1 All ER.

Gillon, R. (ed.) (1986) *Philosophical Medical Ethics.* Chichester: Wiley.

Gokonyo, C. (2008) 'Taking social relationships seriously: lessons learned from the informed consent practices of a vaccine trial on the Kenyan coast', *Social Science & Medicine*, 67, 5: 708–720.

Goodenough, T., Williamson, E., Kent, J. and Ashcroft, R. (2003) '"What did you think about that?" Researching children's participation in a longitudinal genetic epidemiological study', *Children and Society*, 17, 2: 113–125.

Goodenough, T., Williamson, E., Kent, J. and Ashcroft, R. (2004) 'Ethical protection in research: including children in debate', in Smyth, M. and Williamson, E. (eds) *Researchers and Their 'Subjects'. Ethics, Power, Knowledge and Consent.* Bristol: Policy Press, pp. 55–72.

Gordon, D., Adelman, L., Ashworth, K., Bradshaw, J., Levitas, R., Middleton, S. et al. (2000) *Poverty and Social Exclusion in Britain.* York: Joseph Rowntree Foundation.

Gordon-Smith, P. (2009) 'The morality of young children in their early years setting', *Childhoods Today.* Available at: http://www.childhoodstoday.org/journal.php (accessed 25 July 2010).

Gorringe, T. (1999) *Fair Shares; Ethics and the Global Economy.* London: Thames & Hudson.

Grodin, M. and Glantz, L. (1994) *Children as Research Subjects: Science Ethics and Law.* New York: Oxford University Press.

Hallowell, N., Lawton J. and Gregory, S. (eds) (2005) *Reflections on Research: The Realities of Doing Research in the Social Sciences.* Maidenhead: Open University Press.

Harcourt, D. and Conroy, H. (2005) 'Informed assent: ethics and processes when researching with young children', *Early Child Development and Care*, 175, 6: 567–577.

Hart, J. and Tyrer, B. (2006) *Research with Children Living in Situations of Armed Conflict: Concepts, Ethics and Methods.* Oxford: Refugee Studies Centre.

Hart, R. (1992) *Children's Participation: From Tokenism to Citizenship.* Paris: UNICEF.

Hart, R. and Lansdown, G. (2002) 'Changing world opens door to children', *CRIN News*, 16: 9–11.

Hastings Center (2002) 'Empirical research on informed consent', *Hastings Center Report Special Supplement*, 29, 1: S1–S42.

Heath, S., Brooks, R., Cleaver, S. and Ireland, E. (2009) *Researching Young People's Lives.* London: Sage Publications.

Helgesson, G. (2005) 'Children, longitudinal studies, and informed consent', *Medicine, Health Care and Philosophy*, 8: 307–313.

Hill, M. (2004) 'Ethical considerations in researching children's experiences', in Greene, S. and Hogan, D. (eds) *Researching Children's Experiences*. London: Sage Publications, pp. 61–86.

HM Treasury, DCSF, DTI and DWP (2003) *Every Child Matters*. London: Stationery Office.

Hood, S. (2002/2004) *The State of London's Children*. London: Office of the Children's Rights Commissioner for London, National Children's Bureau.

Hopkins, P. (2008) 'Ethical issues in research with unaccompanied asylum-seeking children', *Children's Geographies*, 6, 1: 37–48.

Howarth, R. and Hopscotch Asian Women's Centre (1997) *If We Don't Play Now, When Can We?* London: Hopscotch Asian Women's Centre.

Human Rights Act (1998) London: The Stationery Office.

Hutchfield, J. and Coren, E. (forthcoming) 'The child's voice in service evaluation: ethical and methodological issues', *Child Abuse Review*.

ICH (European Agency for the Evaluation of Medicinal Products) (2000) *ICH Topic E11 Note for Guidance on Clinical Investigation of Medicinal Products in the Paediatric Population*. London: CPMP/ICH/27/11/99.

Iltis, A. (2005) *Research Ethics*. Abingdon: Routledge.

Indian Medical Research Council (n.d.) *Guidance for International Collaboration for Research in Biomedical Sciences*. Available at: http://www.icmr.nic.in/guide.htm (accessed 24 February 2010).

International Federation of Journalists (1998) *Children's Rights and the Media: Guidelines and Principles for Reporting on Issues Involving Children*. London: IFJ.

IPCC (InterGovernmental Panel on Climate Change) (2007) *Fourth Report on Global Warming*. Available at: http://www.ipcc.ch (accessed 25 July 2010).

Iphofen, R. (2005) 'Ethical issues in qualitative health research', in Holloway, I. (ed.) *Qualitative Research in Health Care*. Maidenhead: Open University Press, pp. 17–32.

Iphofen, R. (2009) *Ethical Decision Making in Social Research*. Basingstoke: Palgrave Macmillan.

Iphofen, R., Dench, S. and Huws, U. (2004) 'Ethical issues in cross-national research: the RESPECT Project in context', paper presented at the Impact of Social Science Research on Social Policy: Governance and Management, European Cross-National Research and Policy Conference, London, September.

Israel, M. and Hay, I. (2006) *Research Ethics for Social Scientists*. London: Sage Publications.

Jabeen, T. (2009) '"But I've never been asked!" Research with children in Pakistan', *Children's Geographies*, 7, 4: 405–419.

Jaffer, U. and Cameron, A. (2000) 'Deceit and fraud in medical research', *International Journal of Surgery*, 4, 2: 122–126.

James, A. and Prout, A. (eds) (1997) *Constructing and Reconstructing Childhood*. London: Falmer.

John, T., Hope, J., Savulescu, J., Stein, A. and Pollard, A.J. (2008) 'Children's consent and paediatric research: is it appropriate for healthy children to be the decision-makers in clinical research?', *Archives of Disease in Childhood*, 93: 379–383.

Karkara, R. and O'Kane, C. (2002) 'Young citizens for a new era in South and Central Asia', *Children's Rights Information Network News*, 16: 13–14.

Katz, A. (ed.) (2002) *Parenting Under Pressure: Prison*. London: Young Voice.

Kellett, M. and Nind, M. (2001) 'Ethics in quasi-experimental research on people with severe learning difficulties: dilemmas and compromises', *British Journal of Learning Difficulties*, 29: 51–55.

Kellett, M. with Forrest, R., Dent, N. and Ward, S. (2005) 'Just teach us the skills please, we'll do the rest: empowering ten-year-olds as active researchers', *Children & Society*, 18, 5: 329–343.

Kempf, H. (2008) *How the Rich are Destroying the Earth*. Totnes: Green Books.

Kendrick, A., Steckley, L. and Lerpiniere, J. (2008) 'Ethical issues, research and vulnerability: gaining the views of children and young people in residential care', *Children's Geographies*, 6, 1: 79–93.

Kennedy, I. (1988) *Treat Me Right*. Oxford: Clarendon Press.

Kennedy, I. (2001) *The Report of the Independent Inquiries into Paediatric Cardiac Services at the Royal Brompton Hospital and Harefield Hospital*. London: Stationery Office.

Kessel, R. (1989) '(Mis)understanding Cleveland: foundational issues and the sexual abuse of children', *Paediatric and Perinatal Epidemiology*, 3: 347–352.

King, M. and Yuille, J. (1987) 'Suggestibility and the child witness', in Ceci, S., Toglia, M. and Ross, D. (eds) *Children's Eyewitness Memory*. New Yok: Springer-Verlag, pp. 24–35.

Kingsman, S. (1992) 'Periods of anxiety', *Health Education,* 92: 9–12.

Kirby, P., Lanyon, C., Cronin, K. and Sinclair, R. (2003) *Building a Culture of Participation: Involving Children and Young People in Policy, Service Planning, Delivery and Evaluation*. London: DfES.

Knox, C.A. and Burkhart, P.V. (2007) 'Issues related to children participating in clinical research', *Journal of Pediatric Nursing*, 22, 4: 310–318.

Ladd, R. (2003) 'Child assent revisited', *American Journal of Bioethics*, 3, 4: 37–38.

Lancaster, P. and Broadbent, V. (2003) *Listening to Young Children Training Pack*. Buchingham: Open University Press/McGraw Hill.

Laws, S., and Mann, G. (2004) *So You Want to Involve Children in Research? A Toolkit Supporting Children's Meaningful and Ethical Participation in Research Relating to Violence against Children*. Stockholm: Save the Children.

Lawson, E. (1991) 'Are Gillick rights under threat?', *Childright*, 80: 17–21.

Leathard, A. and McLaren, S. (2007) *Ethics*. Bristol: Policy Press.

Lewis A. (2002) 'Accessing, through research interviews, the views of children with difficulties in learning', *Support for Learning*, 17, 3: 110–116.

Lewis, J. (2002) 'Research and development in social care: governance and good practice', *Research Policy and Planning*, 20, 1: 3–9.

Lolichen, P. (2006) *Children's Informed Participation in Governance*. Available at: http://www.workingchild.org (accessed 25 July 2010).

Lolichen, P. (2007) 'Children in the drivers' seat: children conducting a study of their transport and mobility problems', *Children, Youth and Environments*, 17, 1: 238–256.

Lolichen, P., Shetty, A., Shenoy, J. and Nash, C. (2007) 'Children in the driver's seat', *Participatory Learning and Action*, 56: 49–55.

Lukes, S. (2008) *Moral Relativism*. London: Profile Books.

Lynas, M. (2007) *Six Degrees*. London: Fourth Estate.

Mauthner, M., Birch, M., Jessop, J. and Miller, T. (eds) (2002) *Ethics of Qualitative Research*. Buckingham: Open University Press.

Marshall, P. (2007) *Ethical Challenges in Research Design and Informed Consent for Health Research in Resource-Poor Countries*. Geneva: WHO.

Mayall, B. (ed.) (1994) *Children's Childhoods, Observed and Experienced*. London: Falmer.

Mayall, B. (2002) *Towards a Sociology for Childhood*. London: RoutledgeFalmer.

Mayall, B. and Hood, S. (2001) 'Breaking barriers: provision and participation in an Out-of-School Centre', *Children & Society*, 15, 70–81.

Mayor of London (2003) *Towards a child-friendly London. The Mayor's Children and Young People's Strategy*. London: GLA.

McLeod, J. and Thomson, R. (2010) *Researching Social Change: Inventing Adulthoods.* Available at: http://www.lsbu.ac.uk/inventingadulthoods (accessed 10 March 2010).

MRC (Medical Research Council) (2004) *Medical Research Involving Children.* London: MRC.

Melvillle, R. and Urquhart, R. (2002) *Partners in Ethical Dilemmas: On Academics and Practitioners Collaborating.* Sydney: Uniting Care Burnside.

Mertens, D. and Ginsberg, P. (2009) *The Handbook of Social Research Ethics.* London: Sage Publications.

Miller, J . (1996/1998) *Never Too Young: How Young Children Can Take Responsibility and Make Decisions. A Handbook for Early Years Workers.* London: National Early Years Network and Save the Children.

Miller, N. (2002) *Environmental Politics.* New York: Routledge.

Miller, R. (2004a) *Children, Ethics and Modern Medicine.* Bloomington, IN: Indianapolis University Press.

Miller, R. (2004b) In Barnes, C. and Mercer, G. (eds) *Implementing the Social Model of Disability: Theory and Research.* Leeds: The Disability Press, pp. 138–156.

Molyneux, S. and Geissler, P. (2008) 'Ethics and the ethnography of medical research in Africa', *Social Science & Medicine*, 67, 5: 685–695.

Monbiot, G. (2006) *Heat.* London: Penguin.

Schenk, K. and Williamson J. (2005) *Ethical Approaches to Gathering Information from Children and Adolescents in International Settings: Guidelines and Resources.* Washington, DC: Population Council.

Montgomery, H. (2007) 'Working with child prostitutes in Thailand: problems of practice and interpretation', *Childhood*, 14, 4: 415–430.

Montgomery, J. (1992) 'Parents and children in dispute: who has the final word?', *Journal of Child Law*, April: 85–89.

Morris, J. (1998) *Don't Leave Us Out! Involving Disabled Children and Young People with Communication Impairments.* York: Joseph Rowntree Foundation.

Morrow V. (1998) '"If you were a teacher, it would be harder to talk to you": reflections on qualitative research with children in school', *International Journal of Social Research Methodology*, 1, 4: 297–313.

Morrow V. (2001) 'Using qualitative methods to elicit young people's perspectives on their environments: some ideas for community health initiatives', *Health Education Research; Theory and Practice*, 16, 3: 255–268.

Morrow, V. (2005) 'Ethical issues in collaborative research with children', in Farrell, A. (ed.) *Ethical Research with Children.* Buckingham: Open University Press, pp. 150–165.

Morrow, V. (2008) 'Ethical dilemmas in research with children and young people about their social environments', *Children's Geographies*, 6, 1: 49–61.

Morrow, V. (2009) 'The ethics of social research with children and families in Young Lives: practical experiences', *Working Paper No 53.* Oxford: Young Lives. Available at: http://www.younglives.org.uk (accessed 25 July 2010).

Morrow, V. and Richards, M. (1996) 'The ethics of social research with children: an over-view', *Children & Society*, 10: 90–105.

Mudaly, N. and Goddard, G. (2006) *The Truth Is Longer Than a Lie: Children's Experiences of Abuse and Professional Interventions.* London: Jessica Kingsley.

Mudaly, N. and Goddard, G. (2008) 'The ethics of involving children who have been abused in child abuse research', *International Journal of Children's Rights*, 17: 261–281.

Munro, E. (2008) 'Research governance, ethics and access: a case study illustrating the new challenges facing social researchers', *International Journal of Social Research Methodology*, 11, 5: 429–439.

Murray, C. (2005) 'Children and young people's participation and non-participation in research', *Adoption and Fostering*, 29, 1: 57–66.

Murray, K. (1988) *Evidence from Children*. Edinburgh: Scottish Law Commission.

NCB (National Children's Bureau) (2003) *Guidelines for Research*. London: NCB. Available at: http://www.ncb.org.uk/ourwork/research_guidelines.pdf (accessed 18 February 2004).

NCH (National Children's Homes) (2001a) *Participating in Good Practice: A Resource Pack to Support User Participation in NCH Projects*. London: NCH.

NCH (2001b) *Positive Image: NCH Photographic Guidelines*. London: NCH.

NIH (National Institutes of Health) (2007) http://www.cirp.org/library/ethics/nuremberg (accessed 25 July 2010).

Nicholson, R. (ed.) (1986) *Medical Research with Children: Ethics, Law and Practice*. Oxford: Oxford University Press.

Neill, S. (2005) 'Research with children: a critical review of the guidelines', *Journal of Child Health Care*, 9, 1: 46–58.

Noyes, J. (1999) *The Voices and Choices of Children on Long-term Ventilation*. London: Stationery Office.

Nuffield Council on Bioethics (1999) *The Ethics of Clinical Research in Developing Countries*. London: Nuffield Foundation.

Nuffield Council on Bioethics (2005) *The Ethics of Research Related to Healthcare in Developing Countries*. London: Nuffield Foundation.

Nuremberg Code (1947) Available at: http://www.med.umich.edu/irbmed/ethics/Nuremberg/NurembergCode.html (accessed 15 November 2002).

Nyambedha, E.O. (2008) 'Ethical dilemmas of social science research on AIDS and orphanhood in Western Kenya', *Social Science and Medicine*, 67: 771–779.

Oakley, A., Wiggins, M., Turner, H., Rajan, L. and Barker, M. (2003) 'Including culturally diverse samples in health research: a case study of an urban trial of social support', *Ethnicity and Health*, 8, 1: 29–39.

OCRCL (Office of the Children's Rights Commission for London) (2001) *Sort it out!: Report of survey of 3,000 young Londoners*. London: OCRCL.

OCRCL (2002a) *Advisory Board Handbook*. London: OCRCL.

OCRCL (2002b) *Children and Young People's Participation in Decision-Making in London*. London: OCRCL.

O'Kane, C. (2008) 'The development of participatory techniques: facilitating children's views about decisions which affect them', in Christensen, P. and James, A. (eds) *Research with Children*. London: RoutledgeFalmer, pp. 136–159.

Osler, A., Street, C., Lall, M. and Vincent, K. (2002) *Not a Problem? Girls and School Exclusion*. York: Joseph Rowntree Foundation/National Children's Bureau.

Oswin, M. (1971) *The Empty Hours*. Penguin: Harmondsworth.

Parsons, R. (2005) 'Grief stricken: Zimbabwean children in everyday extremity and the ethics of research', *Anthropology Southern Africa*, 28, 3–4: 73–77.

Pearce, F. (2010) *People Quake*. London: Bantam Books.

Percy-Smith, B. and Thomas, N. (2010) *A Handbook of Children and Young People's Participation*. London: Joseph Routledge Foundation.

Phoenix, A. (1991) *Young Mothers?* Cambridge: Polity Press.

Pinson, H., Arnot, M. and Candappa, M. (2010) *Education, Asylum and The 'Non-Citizen' Child: The Politics of Compassion and Belonging*. Basingstoke: Palgrave Macmillan.

Plant, R. (1992) 'Citizenship in rights and welfare', in Coote, A. (ed.) *The Welfare of Citizens*. London: IPPR, pp. 15–30.

Plumwood, V. (2002) *Environmental Culture: The Ecological Crisis of Reason*. London: Routledge.

Porter, G. and Abane, A. (2008) 'Increasing children's participation in transport planning: reflections on methodology in a child-centred research project', *Children's Geographies*, 6, 2: 151–167.

Porter, G., Hampshire, K., Abane, A., Munthali, A., Robson, E. and Mashiri, M. (2010) 'Where dogs, ghosts and lions roam: learning from mobile ethnographies on the journey from school', *Children's Geographies*, 8, 2: 91–105.

Porter, G., Hampshire, K., Bourdillon, M., Robson, E., Munthali, A., Abane, A. and Mashiri, M. (2010) 'Children as research collaborators: issues and reflections from a mobility study in sub-Saharan Africa', *American Journal of Community Psychology*.

Porter, J. and Lewis, A . (2001) *Methodological Issues in Interviewing Children and Young People with Learning Difficulties. ESRC Briefing Paper*. Birmingham: Birmingham University.

Powell, M. and Smith, A. (2006) 'Ethical Guidelines for research with children. Kotuitui', *New Zealand Journal of Social Sciences Online*, 1: 125–138.

Powell, M. and Smith, A. (2009) 'Children's participation rights in research', *Childhood*, 16: 124–142.

Prendergast, S. (1994) *This Is the Time to Grow Up': Girl's Experiences of Menstruation in School*. London: Family Planning Association.

Prendergast, S. (1995) '"With gender on my mind": menstruation and embodiment at adolescence', in Holland, J. and Blair, M. (eds) *Debates and Issues in Feminist Research and Pedagogy*. Buckingham: Open University Press, pp. 196–213.

Price, D. (2008) *Anthropological Intelligence: the Deployment and Neglect of Anthropological Knowledge during the Second World War*. Durham, NC: Duke University Press.

Punch, S. (2002) 'Research with children: the same or different from research with adults?', *Childhood*, 9, 3: 321–341.

Qvortrup, J. (2005) *Studies in Modern Childhood*. Basingstoke: Palgrave.

Qvortrup, J., Bardy, M., Sgritta, G. and Wintersberger, H. (eds) (1994) *Childhood Matters: Social Theory, Practice and Politics*. Aldershot: Avebury.

Redfern, M. (2001) *The Royal Liverpool Children's Hospital Inquiry Report*. London: Stationery Office.

Roberts, I. and Godlee, F. (2007) 'Reducing the carbon footprint of medical conferences', *British Medical Journal*, 334: 324–325.

Robertson, J. and Robertson, J. (1989) *Separation and the Very Young*. London: Free Association Books.

Robson, E. (2001) 'Interviews worth the tears? Exploring dilemmas of research with young carers in Zimbabwe', *Ethics, Place & Environment*, 4, 2: 135–142.

Robson, E., Porter, G. Hampshire, K. and Bourdillon, M. (2009) '"Doing it right?" Working with young researchers in Malawi to investigate children, transport and mobility', *Children's Geographies*, 7, 4: 467–480.

Robson, S. (2009) 'Producing and using video data in the early years: ethical questions and practical consequences in research with young children', *Children & Society*, online early view.

RCPCH (Royal College of Paediatrics and Child Health) (1992/2000) 'Guidelines for the ethical conduct of medical research involving children', *Archives of Disease in Childhood*, 82: 177–182.

RCP (Royal College of Physicians) (1986) *Research on Healthy Volunteers*. London: RCP.

RCP (1990) *Guidelines on the Practice of Ethics Committees in Medical Research Involving Human Subjects*. London: RCP.

RCP (1990a) *Research Involving Patients*. London: RCP.

Ross, L.F. (2006) *Children in Medical Research: Access Versus Protection*. New York: Oxford University Press.

Samaritans (2008) *Media Guidelines*. Stirling: Samaritans.

Save the Children (1997) *Learning from Experience: Participatory Approaches in SCF*. London: Save the Children.

Save the Children (1999) *We Have Rights Okay!* London: Save the Children.

Save the Children (2007) *Why Social Corporate Responsibility is Failing Children*. London: SCF.

Schenk, K. and Williamson, J. (2005) *Ethical Approaches to Gathering Information from Children and Adolescents in International Settings: Guidelines and Resources*. Washington, DC: Population Council.

Scott, J., Wishart, J. and Bowyer, D. (2006) 'Do current consent and confidentiality requirements impede or enhance research with children with learning disabilities?', *Disability & Society*, 21, 3: 273–287.

Scottish Law Commission (1988) *The Evidence of Children and Other Potentially Vulnerable Witnesses*. Edinburgh: SLC.

Sharav, V. (2003) 'Children in clinical research: a conflict of moral values', *American Journal of Bioethics*, 3, 1: 1–99.

Shiva, A. (2000) *Tomorrow's Biodiversity*. London: Thames & Hudson.

Sime, D. (2008) 'Ethical and methodological issues in engaging young people living in poverty with participatory research methods', *Children's Geographies*, 6, 1: 63–78.

Skelton, T. (2008) 'Research with children and young people: exploring the tensions between ethics, competence and participation', *Children's Geographies*, 6, 1: 21–36.

Slesser, A. and Qureshi, Y. (2009) 'The implications of fraud in medical and scientific research', *World Journal of Surgery*, 33, 11: 2355–2359.

Smart, C., Neale, B. and Wade, A. (2001) *The Changing Experiences of Childhood: Families and Divorce*. Cambridge: Polity.

Smith, F. and Barker, J. (1999) *Child Centred After School and Holiday Care, Final Report to the ESRC*. Hillingdon: University of Brunel.

Smith, F. and Barker, J. (2002) 'School's out', in Edwards, R. (ed.) *Children, Home and School*. London: RoutledgeFalmer, pp. 57–74.

Smith, R., Monaghan, M. and Broad, B (2002) 'Involving young people as researchers: facing up to the methodological issues', *Qualitative Social Work*, 1, 2: 191–207.

Smyth, M. and Williamson, E. (eds) (2004) *Researchers and the 'Subjects': Ethics, Power and Consent*. Bristol: Policy Press.

Social Policy Association (2009) *Guidelines on Research Ethics*. London: SPA.

Solberg, A. (1997) 'Negotiating childhood', in James, A. and Prout, A. (eds) *Constructing and Reconstructing Childhood*. Basingstoke: Falmer Press, pp. 126–144.

Stainton-Rogers, R. and Stainton-Rogers, W. (1992) *Stories of Childhood: Shifting Agendas in Child Concern*. Hemel Hempstead: Harvester.

Stalker, K. (1998) 'Some ethical and methodological issues in research with people with learning difficulties', *Disability and Society*, 1: 5–19.

Stanley, B. and Sieber, J. (eds) (1992) *Social Research on Children and Adolescents: Ethical Iissues*. Thousand Oaks, CA: Sage Publications.

Stephens, P. (2006) *Contemporary Environmental Politics*. Abingdon: Routledge.

Streuli, N. (2010) 'A study of how Peruvian children involved in a social protection programme experience well-being and poverty', unpublished PhD thesis, Institute of Education, University of London.

Sustainable Trials Study Group (2007) 'Towards sustainable clinical trials', *British Medical Journal*, 334: 671–672.

Swift, A. (1997) *Children for Social Change: Education for Citizenship of Street and Working Children in Brazil*. Nottingham: Educational Heretics.

Tafere, Y., Abebe, W. and Assazinew, A. (2009) 'Young Lives Ethiopia qualitative fieldwork 2 data gathering report', Young Lives internal document. Oxford: Young Lives.

Tarling, R. (2006) *Managing Social Research: A Practical Guide.* London: Routledge.

Thomas, N. and O'Kane, C. (1998) 'The ethics of participatory research with children', *Children and Society*, 12, 5, 336–348.

Thomson, R. (2007) 'The qualitative longitudinal case history: practical, methodological and ethical reflections', *Social Policy & Society*, 6, 4: 571–582.

Thomson, R. (2008) *Unfolding Lives: Youth, Gender and Change.* Bristol: Policy Press.

Tisdall, K., Davis, J. and Gallagher, M. (2009) *Researching with Children and Young People.* London: Sage Publications.

Turtle, K., McElearney, A. and Scott, J. (2010) 'Involving children in the design and development of research instruments and data collection procedures: a case study in primary schools in Northern Ireland', *Child Care in Practice*, 16, 1: 57–82.

Twum–Danso, A. (2010) 'The construction of childhood in Ghana', in Percy-Smith, B. and Thomas, N. (eds) *A Handbook of Children and Young People's Participation.* London: Joseph Routledge Foundation, pp. 133–140.

Twum Danso, A. (2009) 'Situating participatory methodologies in context: the impact of culture on adult–child interactions in research and other projects', *Children's Geographies*, 7, 4: 379–389.

UK Government (2007) *Report to the UN Committee on the Rights of the Child.* London: DCSF.

United Nations (1989) *Convention on the Rights of the Child.* New York: UNHCHR.

United Nations (2009) *World Population Report.* New York: UN.

United Nations Committee on the Rights of the Child (1995, 2003, 2008) *Consideration of Reports Submitted by States Parties Under Article 44 of the Convention, Concluding Observations: United Kingdom of Great Britain and Northern Ireland.* Geneva: United Nations. Available at: http://www2.onchr.org (accessed 25 July 2010).

United States Department of Health & Human Sciences (n.d.) 'Special protections for children as research subjects'. Available at: http://www.hhs.gov/ohrp/children/ (accessed 24 February 2010).

Vakaoti, P. (2009) 'Researching street-frequenting young people in Suva (Fiji): ethical considerations and impacts', *Children's Geographies*, 7, 4: 435–450.

Van Beers, H. (2002) 'Pushing the participation agenda – experiences from Africa', *Children's Rights Information Network News*, 16: 19–20.

Vennam, U. and Komanduri, A. (2009) 'Young Lives India qualitative fieldwork 2 data gathering report', Internal document. Oxford: Young Lives.

Verhaeghe, P. (2007) Health4Life conference. Available at: http://www.dcu.ie/health4-life/conferences/2007 (accessed 10 March 2010).

Vernon, T. (1980) *Gobbledegook.* London: NCC.

Walsh, K. (2005) 'Researching sensitive issues', in Farrell, A. (ed.) *Ethical Research with Children.* Buckingham: Open University Press, pp. 68–80.

Ward, L. (1997) *Seen and Heard: Involving Disabled Children and Young People in Research and Development Projects.* York: Joseph Rowntree Foundation.

Wendler, D., Rackoff, J., Emanuel, E. and Grady, G. (2002) 'Commentary: the ethics of paying for children's participation in research', *Journal of Pediatrics*, 141, 2: 166–171.

Williamson, E., Goodenough, T., Kent, J. and Ashcroft, R. (2005) 'Conducting research with children: the limits of confidentiality and child protection protocols', *Children & Society*, 19, 5: 397–409.

Willett, R. (2009a) '"As soon as you get on Bebo you just go mad": young consumers and the discursive construction of teenagers online', *Young Consumers: Insight and Ideas for Responsible Marketers*, 10, 4: 283–296.

Willett, R. (2009b) '"It feels like you've grown up a bit": Bebo and teenage identity', ESRC seminar series: The educational and social impact of new technologies on young people in Britain. Seminar Four, 2 March, LSE, London. Available at: http://www.education. ox.ac.uk/esrcseries/publications/index.php (accessed 25 July 2010).

Willow, C. (1997) *Hear! Hear! Promoting Children's and Young People's Democratic Participation in Government.* London: Local Government Information Unit.

Willow, C., Marchant, R., Kirby, P. and Neale B. (2004) *Young Children's Citizenship: Ideas Into Practice.* York: Joseph Rowntree Foundation.

Winter, K. (2009) 'Relationships matter: the problems and prospects for social workers' relationships with young children in care', *Child & Family Social Work*, 14: 450–460.

Winter, K. (2010a) 'The perspectives of young children in care: implications for social work practitioners', *Children and Family Social Workers*, 15, 2: 186–195.

Winter, K. (2010b) *Building Relationships and Communicating with Young Children: a Practice Guide for Social Workers.* Abingdon: Routledge.

Woodhead, M. and Faulkner, D. (2000) 'Subjects, objects or participants? Dilemmas of psychological research with children', in Christensen, P. and James, A. (eds) *Research with Children.* London: RoutledgeFalmer, pp. 9–35.

WHO (World Health Organization), Research Ethics Review Committee (n.d.) *Informed Consent Template for Research Involving Children (Qualitative Studies).* Geneva: WHO. Available at: http://www.who.org (accessed 3 March 2010).

WMA (World Medical Association) (1964/2009) *Declaration of Helsinki.* Fernay-Voltaire: World Medical Association.

Young Lives (n.d.) *Memorandum of Understanding for Young Lives Field Researchers.* Oxford: Young Lives. Available at: http://www.younglives.org.uk

Young Lives (2006) *Fieldworker Instruction Handbook.* Oxford: Young Lives. Available at: http://www.younglives.org.uk

Young Lives (2009a) '"Nothing is impossible for me". Stories from Young Lives children'. Oxford: Young Lives. Available at: http://www.younglives.org.uk

Young Lives (2009b) Fieldwork manual. Young Lives internal document. Available at: http://www.younglives.org.uk

Useful websites (last accessed 10 February 2010)

Association of Internet Researchers: http://www.aoir.org/reports/ethics.pdf

American Anthropological Association: http://www.aaanet.org/committees/ethics/ethics-code.pdf

British Psychological Society: Code of Conduct: http://www.bps.org.uk/the-society/code-ofconduct/code-of-conduct_home.cfm

British Sociological Association, Statement of Ethics Practice:
http://www.britsoc.co.uk/equality/Statement+Ethical+Practice.htm

British Educational Research Association, Revised Ethics Guidelines for Educational Research (2004): http://www.bera.ac.uk/blog/category/publications/guidelines/

Higher Education Funding Council for England: http://www.hefce.ac.uk

Social Research Association: Ethics Guidelines:
http://www.the-sra.org.uk/documents/pdfs/ethics03.pdf

The Ethics Guidebook: http://www.ethicsguidebook.ac.uk

Universities and Colleges Employer Association: Safety in Fieldwork, and Health and Safety Guidelines for Working Overseas: http://www.ucea.ac.uk/en/Publications/Health_and_Safety.cfm

USA research ethics guidance connected with international research:
http://bms.brown.edu/fogarty/consent.htm

USA Department of Health & Human Sciences: http://www.hhs.gov/ohrp/children/

Index

3 Ps 132

archiving data 35, 117
assent 102–103, 113–114
Association of Research Ethics Committees
    (AREC) journal 80

beneficial research 106
benefits 24, 26
bioethics 16
book corner (children's view), 121
British Sociological Association (BSA) 31, 140
budgeting research
    financial value of time 70
    grants 141
    payment types 68–69
    payments in context 69–70

carbon costs 66
carbon emissions 64–65
    British policy 65
    small families 65
Chatham House rules 35
children in
    Africa 80–81
    Australia 28–29, 32
    British Commonwealth 103–105
    Ethiopia 3, 38, 70, 71–72, 95, 98, 115
    Europe 102–103
    Fiji 69
    Germany 33–34
    Ghana 119
    Greece 33–34
    Italy 33–34
    India 70, 95, 127
    Kenya 56, 95, 119–120
    Netherlands 43–44
    Nigeria 117–118
    Northern Ireland 46, 53–54
    Peru 69, 70, 95, 98, 117
    Scotland 51, 69
    Sweden 43–44
    Tanzania 28
    Uganda 61

children in *cont.*
    USA 54–55, 102–103, 106–107
    Vietnam 70, 95, 115, 117
    Zimbabwe 28, 71
children 2
    abused 28–29
    carbon costs 66
    caring for 23
    climate change effect 64
    ethical review 136
    ethnographic research 61
    exclusions 50
    as 'guinea pigs' 16
    human becomings 12
    inclusive research 51
    insider 73
    international advocacy 57–59
    outburst comics 54–55
    privacy 37–39
    published reports impact 134–135
    research ethics 4
    respecting 53, 110, 120–121, 137
    rights to information 85
    rights 31, 37
    transferring power to 109
    in UK 58
    viewpoint 12, 14, 53–54, 121
    welfare 29
Children in Scotland 51
Children's Rights Alliance for England
    (CRAE), 58
    in Britain 136
    human rights research 59
    journalists in children's rights 130
competence 100, 105, 108–110
confidentiality 31, 39 (see also 'privacy')
    BSA guidelines 31
    ethical questions 32
    good practice 37
    legal rights 31
    privacy rights 37–38
    pseudonym 39
    research and promises 32
    respect to readers' concern 34–35